ECOLOGY

Britannica Illustrated Science Library

Encyclopædia Britannica, Inc.
Chicago ▪ London ▪ New Delhi ▪ Paris ▪ Seoul ▪ Sydney ▪ Taipei ▪ Tokyo

Britannica Illustrated Science Library

Idea and Concept of This Work: Editorial Sol 90

General Director: Fabián Cassan

Project Management: Carolina Berdiñas

Photo Credits: Comstock/Jupiterimages, Corbis, Getty Images

Composition and Pre-press Services: Editorial Sol 90

Translation Services and Index: Publication Services, Inc.

Britannica Illustrated Science Library Staff

Editorial
Michael Levy, *Executive Editor, Core Editorial*
John Rafferty, *Associate Editor, Earth Sciences*
William L. Hosch, *Associate Editor, Mathematics and Computers*
Kara Rogers, *Associate Editor, Life Sciences*
Rob Curley, *Senior Editor, Science and Technology*
David Hayes, *Special Projects Editor*

Art and Composition
Steven N. Kapusta, *Director*
Carol A. Gaines, *Composition Supervisor*
Christine McCabe, *Senior Illustrator*

Media Acquisition
Kathy Nakamura, *Manager*

Copy Department
Sylvia Wallace, *Director*
Julian Ronning, *Supervisor*

Information Management and Retrieval
Sheila Vasich, *Information Architect*

Production Control
Marilyn L. Barton

Manufacturing
Kim Gerber, *Director*

International Standard Book Number (volume):
978-1-61535-341-5
Britannica Illustrated Science Library: Ecology 2010

Printed in Malaysia/Times Offset

01-012010

www.britannica.com

Ecology

Contents

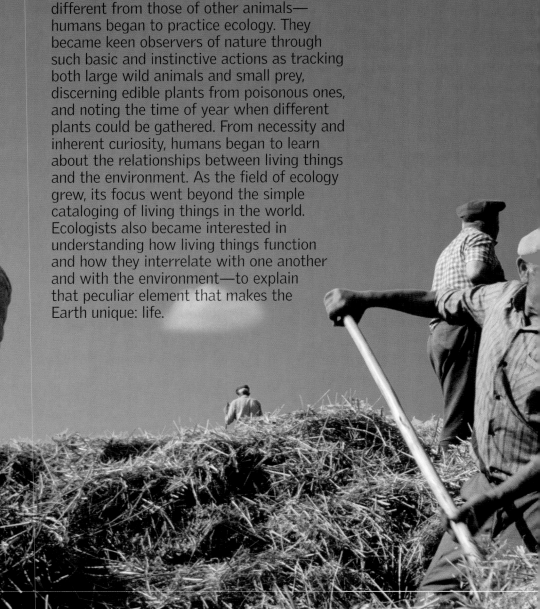

The Oldest Science . . . and the Most Recent

ong ago when people still lived in caves—perhaps at the same time when they developed habits that were different from those of other animals— humans began to practice ecology. They became keen observers of nature through such basic and instinctive actions as tracking both large wild animals and small prey, discerning edible plants from poisonous ones, and noting the time of year when different plants could be gathered. From necessity and inherent curiosity, humans began to learn about the relationships between living things and the environment. As the field of ecology grew, its focus went beyond the simple cataloging of living things in the world. Ecologists also became interested in understanding how living things function and how they interrelate with one another and with the environment—to explain that peculiar element that makes the Earth unique: life.

This unique science was so complex and encompassing that it was not until the 19th century that its scientific foundations could be laid, formal study could begin, and the word "ecology" could come into existence. This book serves as a detailed introduction to the subject.

We will begin by learning what ecology is and what it is not. (At times the word has been used incorrectly as a synonym for environmental protection.) Later, we will look at how living things are classified, before moving into the study of the environments in which they live: the land, water, and air.

The next stop along this journey, filled with exciting information and marvelous illustrations, will be devoted to ordering and organizing the surprising diversity of living organisms on Earth. Living things are first grouped into populations according to their kinship, then into communities according to the spaces they share. The exploration into the ways in which organisms interact will show that some interactions can be very cruel, such as those between predators and prey or those between different species that compete with one another for the same resource. This exploration will also reveal surprising relationships in which species mutually benefit from one another.

We will then be ready to understand how nonliving, physical environments influence, modify, and even determine the characteristics of this complex bundle of interactions. At this moment, we will define the word "ecosystem" and learn how materials and energy pass through its living and nonliving parts. These concepts are needed for the next step, the examination of each of the world's major biomes. We will examine both terrestrial and aquatic biomes and the characteristic plant and animal species found within them, including those species that may be in danger of extinction. Finally, we will look at the place that people occupy in the biosphere—the ways in which their activities change nature and even create new ecosystems. In the urban centers, different species have developed novel strategies to cope with the challenges of life in the "concrete jungle." Despite the damage to the environment caused by human beings, there is a ray of hope: human ingenuity can also be used to protect the environment and to reduce the harm caused by their activities.

Ecology: Introduction and Background

Any landscape, from an arid desert to a rainforest, conceals an astonishing diversity of organisms in action. Each appears to play a role and seems to be busy with some task. How can we understand what takes place in the environment? How can we determine the mechanisms that govern the actions of living things? Understanding ecology is a

monumental task. As a first step, we will investigate the various media in which life occurs—water, land, and air. (Air is as important as land and water, even though it is much less populated.) Then we will classify living things into six major kingdoms, which in general correspond to animals, plants, fungi, archaea, bacteria, and protists. Turn the page to begin your exploration into the world of ecology. ●

What Is Ecology?

Some branches of biology, such as zoology and botany, are dedicated to the study of living things. Other sciences, such as geology and meteorology, deal with the nonliving parts of the environment. These nonliving parts include the composition of the Earth, weather phenomena, and volcanoes. Ecology, however, takes a little from each of these sciences and looks at the interactions among organisms in a community and between the community and the environment. In this way, ecology seeks to explain biodiversity, the distribution of species, and the way ecosystems function. It also endeavors to foresee the consequences that might result from future changes. ●

Levels of Organization

To help understand the complexity of life, ecologists recognize different levels of organization.

A group of individuals of the same species in a given location constitutes a population. The populations of different organisms that share an area and occupy it at the same time make up a community. The community, in contact with the nonliving parts of the environment, forms an ecosystem. All ecosystems taken together comprise the biosphere.

25

The approximate number of chemical elements (out of a total of 92 natural elements) that are used by living things.

40,000

The number of plant species known in the 19th century. About 500,000 are known today.

INDIVIDUAL   POPULATION   COMMUNITY

Relationships

Ecology places a special emphasis on the complex relationships that living things establish within their own species (intraspecific relationships) and between different species in a community (interspecific relationships).

The ants in the photograph hunt together (an intraspecific relationship) and can therefore capture prey that are much larger than any one of the ants. The relationship between the ants and the worm (predation) is interspecific.

Biodiversity

The total number of species of living things that inhabit the planet is unknown. The variety of ways in which they live, however, never ceases to amaze. This diversity can play an important role in the stability of ecosystems.

The leafy sea dragon (*Phycodurus eques*), an exotic relative of sea horses, essentially disappears as it approaches algae; it is hidden by its perfect camouflage.

Recycling

Like energy, nutrients and other substances pass through the living organisms in an ecosystem. In this case, substances are used over and over, creating a cycle.

Earthworms, roundworms, bacteria, and fungi make up a group of organisms known as decomposers. They feed on waste products and on the remains of dead plants and animals. They return nutrients back to the soil, where they are reused by plants.

The Flow of Energy

In studying ecosystems, it is extremely important to determine the way in which energy is transferred from organism to organism.

Energy from the Sun is taken in by plants and passed along to the deer that eat the plants. It eventually reaches the lion, which preys on the deer.

ECOSYSTEM

Distribution

Environmental factors (such as climate, geography, and soil composition) determine the distribution of species in different biomes.

Deserts of ice are among the biomes having the poorest biodiversity. Some of the adaptations of the organisms that live there, however, are surprising.

BIOSPHERE

Milestones in Ecology

Although ecology is usually thought of as one of the newest branches of science, it is also one of the oldest. From the time they were nomadic hunters, people had to be concerned about the relationships between living things.

4th Century BC	19th Century AD	1866	1926	1935	1979
Aristotle and his disciple Theophrastus produce the first writings about the relationships between organisms.	Naturalists embark on great maritime expeditions. Humboldt describes the relationship between living organisms and climate for the first time. Möbius proposes the term biocenosis to refer to the concept that the various species in a community are not independent of one another. Darwin publishes his theory of evolution in *On the Origin of Species*. Warming lays the foundation for a new discipline when he includes a consideration of abiotic (nonliving) factors in the study of communities.	Ernst Haeckel coins the term "ecology" (*oekologie*, in German) and consequently lends recognition to the new discipline.	Vladimir Vernadsky publishes *The Biosphere*. In this book he describes the concept of the biosphere and discusses the principal biogeochemical cycles.	Arthur Tansley coins the term "ecosystem" to refer to the interaction between biocenosis (a group of living beings) and the biotope (the environment in which they live).	James Lovelock publishes *Gaia: A New Vision About Life on Earth*. The author argues that the living and nonliving elements of the planet interact to form a unique organism that regulates itself to maintain conditions that are favorable to life.

The Six Kingdoms

I n order to begin to understand nature, a system must be created to organize the seemingly endless array of organisms. This issue, which has been the topic of many proposals, debates, and disputes among naturalists for centuries, has yet to be completely resolved. Nevertheless, a few methods for classifying organisms have been established that pay attention to the morphological characteristics (or physical features) of different groups and their evolutionary history. Both classification methods are used to determine the relationships between organisms. ●

Universal Names

There are two types of names for organisms. The common name is the one most people use, but common names can vary from one region to another. The scientific name, derived from Latin, allows any researcher in the world to refer to a specific organism without the possibility of confusing one species with another.

The scientific name of the great white shark is *Carcharodon carcharias*.

Amazon river dolphin, pink dolphin, *boto*, and *bufeo* are common names given to a single animal: *Inia geoffrensis*.

BINOMIAL NOMENCLATURE

By convention, scientific names are generally Latin words; they are written in italics.

Inia geoffrensis

The first word is the genus, and its initial letter is always capitalized.

The second word is a qualifier, and together with the first word it indicates the species.

34

The approximate number of phyla into which the animal kingdom is divided. The mollusk phylum alone (which includes snails, octopuses, and clams) has about 90,000 species.

Classifying Life

At one time, all living things were formally classified into two kingdoms, animal and plant. Today the most widely accepted classification divides organisms into six kingdoms, although a few alternative systems have been proposed and are under discussion.

1 ANIMALIA (ANIMALS)

Multicellular organisms. Their cells are eukaryotic and do not have a cell wall. In general, they are able to move under their own power.

1.5 million

The number of species that have been described by science. It might represent only 5% of all the species in the world.

③ PROTISTA (PROTOZOA)

Unicellular and multicellular eukaryotic organisms that are not part of any other kingdom of life. They include euglenoids, dinoflagellates, fungi, and other eukaryotic microorganisms. (In a eukaryote, the cell's genetic material is organized into chromosomes, and a nuclear membrane separates it from the rest of the cell.)

Paramecium sonneborni
Magnified 1,500 times.

② PLANTAE (PLANTS)

Multicellular organisms. Their cells are eukaryotic, and they have a cell wall. Using a pigment called chlorophyll, they capture energy from sunlight and use it to produce and store their food.

④ EUBACTERIA

Unicellular organisms. They are prokaryotes—that is, they have relatively primitive cells. In prokaryotes, genetic material is not surrounded by a nuclear membrane (as it is in eukaryotes); it is instead inside a cytoplasmic compartment.

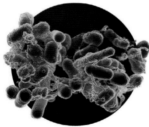

Colony of *Escherichia coli*
Each bacterium is about 100 times smaller than the thickness of a human hair. These bacteria cause various human diseases, such as salmonella.

⑤ FUNGI

Eukaryotic organisms. Traditionally, fungi were included in the plant kingdom, but they now constitute their own group. One of their characteristics is that they form spores. Their cellular structure is very different from that of plants.

Hierarchical Order

Organisms are classified into a system in which some groups are placed within larger groups. For example, domains are divided into kingdoms, which in turn are divided into phyla. Phyla are divided into subphyla and so forth down to the level of species.

An Example: The Classification of Human Beings

Domain:	Eukarya (organisms whose cells contain linear DNA, a cytoskeleton, a nuclear membrane, and other internal membranes).
Kingdom:	Animalia (multicellular organisms that ingest their food).
Phylum:	Chordata (animals that at some time in their life cycle have a hollow dorsal nerve cord and pharyngeal gill slits).
Subphylum:	Vertebrata (animals that have a nerve cord enclosed in a vertebral column).
Superclass:	Tetrapoda (land animals with four limbs).
Class:	Mammalia (the young are nourished with milk from mammary glands; the skin has fur; they are warm-blooded).
Order:	Primates (they have fingers and flat nails, a poor sense of smell, and arboreal habits—or at least their ancestors did).
Family:	Hominidae (bipedal and flat faced, with frontal vision and color vision).
Genus:	Homo (communicates by means of a language). Above, the skulls of three species of the genus Homo are shown.
Species:	Homo sapiens (have a prominent chin, little body hair, and a high forehead).

Homo neanderthalensis

Homo erectus

Homo sapiens

A NEW CLASSIFICATION

The best way of classifying organisms continues to be debated. A new category that has been proposed—the domain—lies above the level of kingdoms. According to this classification scheme, there are three domains (two for prokaryotes and one for eukaryotes), which in turn are divided into kingdoms.

Determining Kinship

Through the study of evolution, it is possible to determine the relatedness and common ancestry of organisms that look very different.

Homologous Structures

They can be equivalent structures (such as the wings of a bat and the wings of a bird) or different structures (such as the wing of a bird and the arm of a human). Nevertheless, they have a common origin and thus denote a degree of kinship.

Analogous Structures

Although these structures appear to be similar or equivalent, a careful analysis will show that they have independent origins (such as the wing of a bird and the wing of an insect). They are simply the result of similar adaptations by organisms to a given environment.

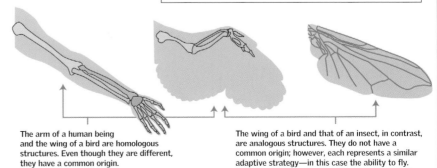

The arm of a human being and the wing of a bird are homologous structures. Even though they are different, they have a common origin.

The wing of a bird and that of an insect, in contrast, are analogous structures. They do not have a common origin; however, each represents a similar adaptive strategy—in this case the ability to fly.

Although they are different, birds and humans are more closely related than birds and insects.

The Soil

A ny study about nature needs to consider the importance of soil. Soil provides the surface upon which terrestrial organisms carry out their existence, and it is typically the first and foremost source of nutrients in an ecosystem. Not all soils are the same, however, nor do they have the same properties. An effort toward understanding the soil will yield surprising details about the world that exists under our feet. ●

One Name, Many Horizons

Below the surface of the ground, the soil is organized into layers (horizons), the structure, composition, and thickness of which depend on many factors in its formation—mineral types, climate, organisms that live in it, and the passage of time. Together, the soil horizons lie upon solid rock (bedrock).

1 A Horizon

This is the top layer of soil, where humus accumulates. Humus is formed from organic material mixed with the mineral components of the soil, and it supports a rich variety of microscopic organisms. When it rains, water dissolves some of the components of the A horizon and carries them into the layer below.

2 B Horizon

This layer has more clay and is rich in minerals, especially iron oxides and lime. It receives material from both the A horizon and the C horizon.

3 C Horizon

Although its characteristics are similar to the B horizon, this layer contains fragments of bedrock that have not been weathered like those in the B horizon.

4 R Horizon

Also known as bedrock, or consolidated rock, it is the solid layer upon which the rest of the soil rests. It slowly contributes mineral material to the layers above it.

500 years

The time required to form a layer of fertile soil 1 inch (2.4 cm) thick.

— Humus

Each horizon can be divided into layers and subhorizons, depending on the soil's particular characteristics.

From Rock to Soil

The formation of the soil is a long process that normally takes thousands of years. Some soils in India, Africa, and Australia are more than two million years old. The process begins with the interaction between the atmosphere and solid rock; then a biological component is added.

SUNSHINE   RAIN

1 Solid rock exposed to the atmosphere begins to weather and erode.

2 Organic material filters into the cracks and helps disintegrate the rock.

HUMUS

3 Organic material, together with minerals from the rock, begin to form a layer of humus. The soil horizons become defined.

4 The soil has formed and begins to develop further. The growth of vegetation deepens the humus layer.

Properties

Because of their nature, soils have a variety of physical and chemical properties. The following are the most important:

COLOR

One of the most useful and readily apparent properties for identifying soil classes is their color.

Black
Black soil is generally associated with a high content of organic material and has good structure. In general it is very fertile.

Red
Red soil is typically rich in iron oxides. It is usually associated with warm climates with low moisture and is low in fertility.

Yellow
Yellow soil tends to have average or low fertility.

Brown
Brown soil has little organic material, and its fertility is variable.

White
White soil is associated with light-colored minerals (such as calcite, gypsum, silicates, and salts). It sometimes indicates soil removal.

Gray
A gray soil is likely one that was saturated with water and in which there was bacterial activity in the absence of oxygen.

TEXTURE

Using a magnifying glass or microscope, it is possible to see that the soil is made up of countless particles of various sizes. This characteristic is extremely important because it determines the soil's porosity, its capacity for aeration, and its ability to hold water.

Soil particles are classified by size.

Sand

Silt

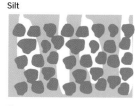

Clay

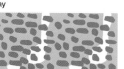

This triangular table can be used to identify soil textures according to the soil's physical composition.

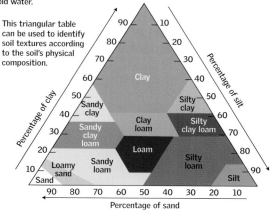

An average volume of soil is primarily composed of mineral particles, air, and water and is only 5% organic material.

Organic material	**5%**
Composed of	
Organisms	10%
Roots	10%
Humus	80%

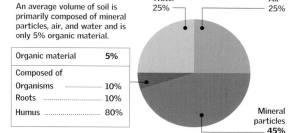

Water 25%
Air 25%
Mineral particles 45%

ACIDITY

The acidity or alkalinity of the soil is another extremely important characteristic. It is measured chemically.

0 Acid — 7 Neutral — 14 Alkaline

Soils with a pH of 7 are neutral. Those with a pH less than 7 are acidic, and those with a pH greater than 7 are alkaline. Typically, agricultural soils are slightly acidic, with a pH between 5.5 and 6.5.

170

The number of colors in which soils can appear.

Miniature Universe

In the soil—within the humus and among the remains of dead plants and animals—there exists a universe of microorganisms that take care of decomposing these materials into simple organic compounds and returning them to the soil.

one billion

The number of animals that can live in 35 cubic feet (1 cubic meter) of fertile soil.

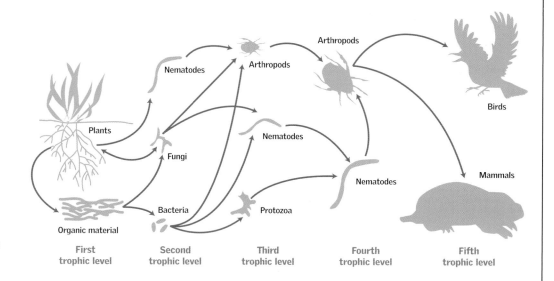

First trophic level
Second trophic level
Third trophic level
Fourth trophic level
Fifth trophic level

Plants, Nematodes, Arthropods, Arthropods, Birds, Fungi, Nematodes, Bacteria, Protozoa, Nematodes, Mammals, Organic material

Water and Air

The existence of life as we know it would scarcely be possible without the presence of water. This marvellous and surprising substance covers about 70% of the Earth's surface, and it typically makes up most of a living organism's body. Air, for its part, is the great provider of oxygen for life, and it has a predominant role in climate, erosion, geography, and, consequently, in the distribution of species. The understanding of the properties of water and air is fundamental to the study of the biosphere. ●

ABSORPTION OF LIGHT

The absorption of light in water—together with the water's salinity—largely determines the kind of life that can be found in aquatic environments. The richest abundance of life is found within about a dozen feet, or several meters, of the water's surface, which is where the penetration of sunlight is greatest. Below a depth of 820 feet (250 m), it is almost completely dark.

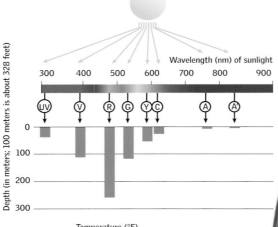

TEMPERATURE

Another very important factor in aquatic environments is water temperature. In the oceans, temperature decreases with depth, but this decrease is not entirely gradual. As one descends from a depth of about 490 feet (150 m), where the solar radiation is very weak, there is a transition zone where temperature drops abruptly called the thermocline. The decrease in temperature with depth becomes gradual again below a depth of about 3,300 feet (1,000 m).

SALINITY

Seawater and bodies of water on land differ in their salinity. The main type of salt in seawater is sodium chloride (table salt), whereas calcium bicarbonate generally predominates in bodies of freshwater. The map shows the salinity of surface ocean water in parts per million.

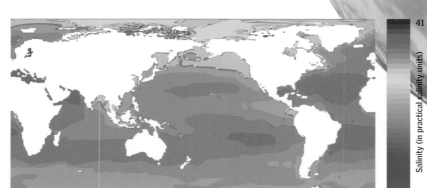

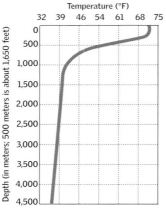

20,000 feet (6,000 m)

The approximate maximum altitude at which life can exist. Above this altitude few organisms can withstand the extreme conditions of temperature, pressure, and lack of oxygen.

Attributes of the Air

From an ecological perspective, air ecosystems do not exist since the organisms that have colonized the air need soil and water to develop. Nevertheless, the atmosphere is vitally important in all the processes that affect life on the planet.

Special adaptations
Organisms have developed adaptations such as feathers, low body density and weight, and specialized appendages in order to fly and make use of the aerial environment.

Wind
Wind, which is a characteristic phenomenon of the aerial environment, exercises a strong influence on terrestrial and aquatic ecosystems because of its effect on the weather—particularly on temperature and moisture levels—and its role in the development of ocean currents. The wind can also carry animals, seeds, and nutrients between distant places.

Moisture
The air holds water vapor, and it helps distribute the water needed by terrestrial organisms.

Erosion
The processes of erosion modify the landscape by wearing away landforms. It also influences the distribution of certain nutrients.

Supply of air
The atmosphere contains gases that animals, plants, and microorganisms need to live.

Protection
The Earth's atmosphere contains a layer of ozone that protects life on Earth from the Sun's harmful ultraviolet radiation. It also contains greenhouse gases that moderate the temperature of the Earth's surface, and it serves as a kind of shield that prevents many meteors from space from reaching the Earth's surface.

TEMPERATURE
One of the most important variables that affect life on Earth is temperature. Although the temperature of the atmosphere generally varies with altitude, the thermal profile of the air immediately above the Earth's surface is determined by many factors.

ATMOSPHERIC PRESSURE
Technically, this is the weight of the air pressing down on the Earth's surface. The pressure of the atmosphere decreases with altitude, which requires special adaptations by numerous organisms that live in high-altitude environments. Atmospheric pressure also plays a fundamental role in the formation of winds.

Meteorologists connect points of equal atmospheric pressure with lines called isobars to analyze weather conditions.

THE OZONE HOLE
In the spring the ozone layer over each polar region undergoes a drastic reduction in density. Such "ozone holes" are causes for concern and they are worsened by industrial emissions of chlorofluorocarbon gases.

COMPOSITION OF THE AIR

Oxygen 20.9%
Gas that is used by most living organisms for respiration.

Secondary gases 0.3%
The atmosphere contains other, less-common gases such as carbon dioxide, methane, hydrogen, and noble gases such as helium, krypton, and neon.

Argon 0.9%
A noble, inert gas that is used in lighting because of its ability to glow brightly when an electric current passes through it.

Nitrogen 78%
Essential element for plant growth.

MARS
Although the constituent gases in the atmosphere of Mars are similar to those in the Earth's atmosphere, their proportions are very different. As a consequence, the atmosphere of Mars cannot support complex life, although there might be some simple life forms, such as certain bacteria, that could withstand its extreme conditions.

Carbon dioxide	95.32%
Nitrogen	2.7%
Argon	1.6%
Oxygen	0.13%

Studying Nature

N ature functions in a delicate equilibrium that has evolved over millions of years. If we eliminate a major predator (such as tigers or white sharks), its prey, instead of prospering, can also become endangered, and the entire ecosystem can undergo changes. An ecosystem involves the flow of energy and materials through both its

HONEYBEES IN ACTION
Colonies of honeybees have disappeared in an
alarming fashion because of a little-understood
phenomenon called colony-collapse disorder.
These insects are responsible for pollinating
many kinds of plants, including many fruits
and vegetables.

living and nonliving parts. Ecologists
organize living things into populations
and communities to help understand this
equilibrium. They study the relationships
between populations and communities.

Taking into account the environment in
which the organisms live, they work
with ecosystems to examine how
everything works together as a
single mechanism. ●

Population

F or biologists, a population is a group of individuals that coexist in space and time, interact with each other, and interbreed. The study of population dynamics is fundamental to the deeper understanding of complex ecosystems. In addition, the collection of population data related to the density, mortality, distribution, and life status of species used for food (such as fish) or industry (such as trees) makes it possible to manage the resource in a rational and responsible manner. ●

Characteristics of Populations

Population studies cover many topics. Investigations examine the distribution of individuals and the ways in which they organize themselves. In addition, population studies involve the development of growth curves and research into the factors that limit growth.

LIFE AND DEATH, ARRIVAL AND DEPARTURE

Among the principal indicators of the behavior of a given population are the birth and death rates and rates of immigration and emigration. These parameters help to determine whether a population is increasing or decreasing.

If the birth rate and immigration rate are greater than the death rate and the rate of emigration, the population increases.

DISTRIBUTION

The individuals of a population in a given environment may be distributed in three different ways, which ultimately depend on the balancing of the effects that tend to bring individuals together or to scatter them.

Random
The distribution is irregular. The location of one individual does not affect the rest.

Uniform
Individuals are scattered in a uniform, or even, manner. Consequently, the presence of one does not diminish the probability of finding another nearby.

Grouped
Individuals are found in groups (such as flocks or swarms). The presence of one individual therefore increases the probability of finding another nearby.

DENSITY

The density of a population is the number of individuals that exist in a given unit area (of a surface). If the size of a population falls below a certain value, the population could disappear.

This graph shows population counts for the Argentine hake (*Merluccius hubbsi*) in the north Argentine Sea (the continental shelf adjacent to Argentina). The population—measured in terms of tonnage—has fallen below a critical minimum because of overfishing. As a result, the population is at risk of collapsing.

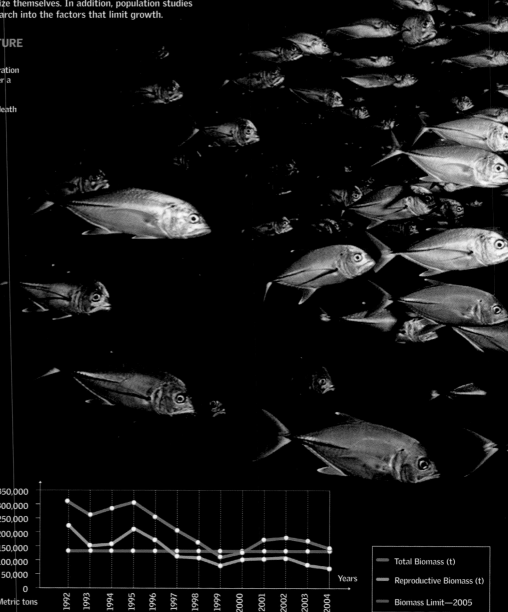

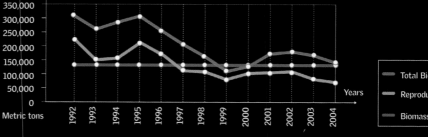

- Total Biomass (t)
- Reproductive Biomass (t)
- Biomass Limit—2005

Intraspecific Relationships

The individuals of the same species within a population interrelate in different ways. Various forms of competition and cooperation have repercussions for the general development of the group.

TERRITORIALITY

Individuals tend to isolate themselves and impose control over a territory in order to avoid overexploitation of the territory's resources. As shown in the picture, a study concerning the division of territory among several species of birds showed that the individuals of the same species never occupied the same space. Individuals of different species, however, were able to share a given territory because they used different resources.

Blue tit

Other birds

Blue tit

Other birds

The blue tit (*Parus caeruleus*) shares its territory with birds of other species but not with other blue tits.

GREGARIOUSNESS

Some animal species tend to gather in groups. Such groupings can be temporary or permanent, and their degree of bonding can vary. In general, these associations assist the group in the hunt for food and in protection, migration, and the care of offspring. Examples of groups include families, colonies (as in the case of corals), and societies, such as those formed by ants and bees.

Some insects (such as termites, ants, and bees) organize themselves into societies where each individual fulfills a determined role. If left outside this society, the individual will perish within hours.

The Limiting Factor

The growth potential of a population is usually very high, but it always encounters obstacles in the form of limiting factors. Such limiting factors might be the exhaustion of a food source, an abrupt change in climate, or the presence of a predator.

EXPONENTIAL GROWTH

When a population colonizes a new environment that is not saturated with members of the same species, it can undergo exponential growth—that is, a growth in the population of the species that is independent of density. If the limiting factor is the availability of resources, then the population will experience an increase in mortality as the resources are used up. As shown in the graph, sometimes this is a cyclical process.

Number of individuals

Time

LOGISTIC GROWTH

Logistic growth is what occurs in most species. The rate of growth is exponential in the beginning. Once the carrying capacity (K—the maximum number of individuals that a given environment can support) is reached, the population becomes stable. It can fluctuate, however, above and below the carrying capacity.

K

Number of individuals

Time

40 square miles (100 sq km)

The area that a male puma (*Puma concolor*) can claim as its own and into which it will not allow another male puma to enter.

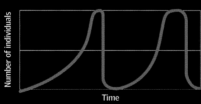

5.6 trillion

The number of descendents that a single female common fly (*Musca domestica*) would have after one year—in a total of seven generations—assuming that they all live.

Community

A population is defined as a collection of individuals of the same species that share a physical space and that are capable of reproducing with each other. The community is a collection of populations of different species that share a common environment and interact with each other. The study of a community reveals a web of complex interactions among species. Each species needs to develop various strategies to defend its area to prevent it from disappearing from the community. ●

The Neighborhood

The relationships that are established among the populations that make up a community can be extremely complex and varied. Almost all of them, however, can be placed into one of three categories: predation, symbiosis, or competition.

Predation

Is the ingestion of an organism by another organism—that is, animals by animals, plants by animals, and animals by plants (in the case of carnivorous plants).

The populations of predators and prey mutually regulate each other. When the hunt becomes more aggressive, the number of prey declines. As this occurs, the predator leaves fewer descendants, because the amount of prey available tends to be the limiting factor. Likewise, once there are fewer predators, the prey population is allowed to recover.

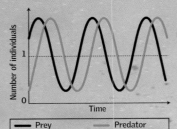

Number of individuals

1

0

Time

— Prey   — Predator

The "war" between predators and prey leads to a refinement of hunting techniques and defensive methods on the part of the contenders. Among the most surprising means of defense is camouflage. Camouflage is exhibited by some species, such as brimstone (*Gonepteryx rhamni*), shown here.

Scientific experiments demonstrate that the presence of predators promotes biodiversity. Furthermore, predators help to ensure that descendants in prey species are among the strongest and fittest specimens. Stronger and fitter prey promote a similar change in predator species.

68 miles (110 km) per hour

The speed that a cheetah (*Acinonyx jubatus*) can reach while hunting. It is the fastest land animal in the world.

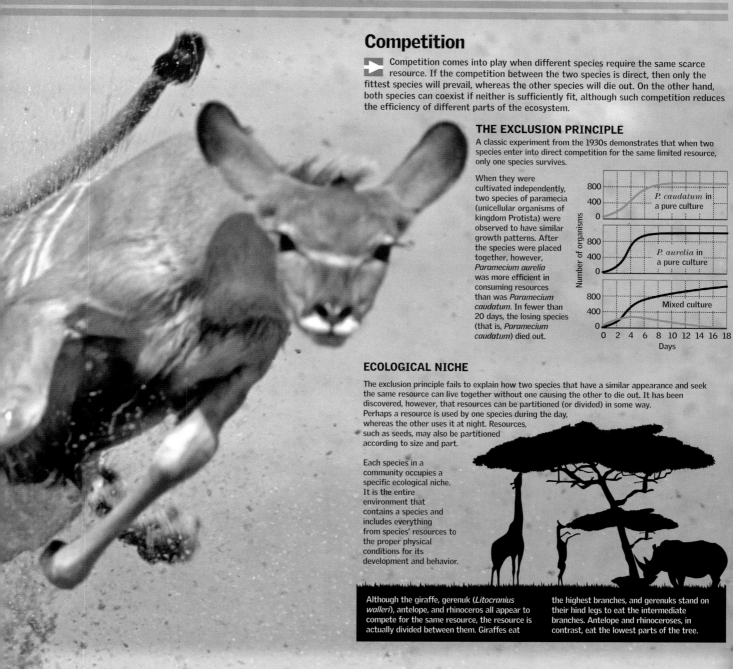

Competition

Competition comes into play when different species require the same scarce resource. If the competition between the two species is direct, then only the fittest species will prevail, whereas the other species will die out. On the other hand, both species can coexist if neither is sufficiently fit, although such competition reduces the efficiency of different parts of the ecosystem.

THE EXCLUSION PRINCIPLE

A classic experiment from the 1930s demonstrates that when two species enter into direct competition for the same limited resource, only one species survives.

When they were cultivated independently, two species of paramecia (unicellular organisms of kingdom Protista) were observed to have similar growth patterns. After the species were placed together, however, *Paramecium aurelia* was more efficient in consuming resources than was *Paramecium caudatum*. In fewer than 20 days, the losing species (that is, *Paramecium caudatum*) died out.

P. caudatum in a pure culture

P. aurelia in a pure culture

Mixed culture

Number of organisms

800 · 400 · 0

800 · 400 · 0

800 · 400 · 0

0 2 4 6 8 10 12 14 16 18
Days

ECOLOGICAL NICHE

The exclusion principle fails to explain how two species that have a similar appearance and seek the same resource can live together without one causing the other to die out. It has been discovered, however, that resources can be partitioned (or divided) in some way. Perhaps a resource is used by one species during the day, whereas the other uses it at night. Resources, such as seeds, may also be partitioned according to size and part.

Each species in a community occupies a specific ecological niche. It is the entire environment that contains a species and includes everything from species' resources to the proper physical conditions for its development and behavior.

Although the giraffe, gerenuk (*Litocranius walleri*), antelope, and rhinoceros all appear to compete for the same resource, the resource is actually divided between them. Giraffes eat the highest branches, and gerenuks stand on their hind legs to eat the intermediate branches. Antelope and rhinoceroses, in contrast, eat the lowest parts of the tree.

Symbiosis

When two species join in permanent relationship, the relationship is called a symbiosis. In some cases, both species benefit. In other cases, one species benefits at the expense of the other.

MUTUALISM

Both species benefit.

The relationship between bees and plants is beneficial for both. The bees obtain food from the plants, and pollen carried by the bees is used to pollinate the flowers of the plants.

PARASITISM

The parasite species benefits at the expense of its host.

Some species of fungus feed on living beings (plants, animals, and even human beings).

COMMENSUALISM

One species benefits; however, the other species neither benefits nor is harmed.

The remoras adhere to the body of a shark and eat the scraps of food left over after the shark feeds on its prey.

Ecosystems

Ecosystems include the populations of living things that make up a community and their interactions with the nonliving elements of the environment (the biotope). Although each ecosystem is uniquely variable and complex, all ecosystems exhibit two conditions: (1) a unidirectional flow of energy that originates with the Sun and permits all the various organisms to live and develop and (2) a cyclic flow of various materials. These materials, such as nutrients, originate in the environment, pass through organisms in the environment, and return once again to the environment. ●

THE SUN
is the principal source of energy on the planet. Life would be impossible without the Sun. Solar energy is used by primary producers (plants and algae) to store chemical energy in the form of sugars.

Food Webs and Energy Flows

True food webs are established in each ecosystem. There are primary producers, primary and secondary consumers, and decomposers. The energy flow in such food webs begins with the Sun.

Every time energy passes from one trophic level to another, there are important losses. Each consumer gains only 10% of the energy that resides in its prey.

PRIMARY PRODUCERS
Plants on land and algae in the water take solar energy and transform it into chemical energy. They make up the first trophic level in the food web.

DECOMPOSERS
These organisms (such as fungi, worms, bacteria, and other microorganisms) are specialized to make use of the sources of energy (such as cellulose and nitrogen compounds) that cannot be used by other animals. Decomposers feed on detritus and other waste products, such as feces and dead animals. As they consume these materials, decomposers return ingredients that circulate in the food web to the environment as new inorganic material.

0.1%

The amount of solar energy reaching the Earth's surface that is used by living things.

PRIMARY CONSUMERS
These consumers are the herbivores that eat the primary producers. Primary consumers require part of the chemical energy that they derive from primary producers to live. Another part is stored within their bodies, and a third part is eliminated without being used.

The Nitrogen Cycle

Nitrogen is a critical element for life. Without it, plants could not live, and thus animals could not exist. Air is made up of 70% nitrogen, but plants cannot use it in its gaseous form. Plants can only take in certain nitrogen compounds found in the soil.

1 Dead animals and the waste products of living animals contain nitrogen that some bacteria and fungi can convert into ammonia (NH_3) and ammonium (NH_4).

2 Other kinds of bacteria convert these compounds into nitrites (NO_2^-). Nitrites are toxic to plants.

3 Other kinds of bacteria convert some of the nitrites into nitrates (NO_3^-). Nitrates are absorbed by plants and used for growth.

4 Plant cells also convert the nitrates into ammonium. Ammonium can be combined with carbon to make amino acids, proteins, and other compounds needed by the plants.

5 Animals obtain nitrogen by eating plants. This nitrogen is eventually returned to the soil.

6 Losses: A large portion of the nitrogen is lost from the cycle. Human activity, fire, and water can remove nitrogen from the ecosystem. Some bacteria convert nitrogen in the soil to nitrogen gas, which escapes into the atmosphere.

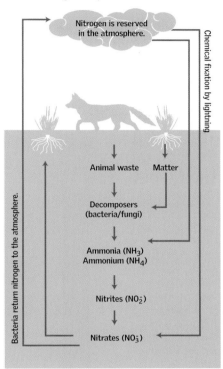

Nitrogen is reserved in the atmosphere.

Chemical fixation by lightning

Bacteria return nitrogen to the atmosphere.

Animal waste | Matter

Decomposers (bacteria/fungi)

Ammonia (NH_3)
Ammonium (NH_4)

Nitrites (NO_2^-)

Nitrates (NO_3^-)

The Carbon Cycle

Carbon is a basic constituent of all organic compounds. The most important source of carbon for living organisms is carbon dioxide (CO_2), which makes up almost 0.04% of the air.

1 Carbon dioxide is incorporated into living things by means of plant photosynthesis. Plants use photosynthesis to form organic compounds. In addition, plants expel carbon dioxide through respiration.

2 Herbivores ingest the organic compounds made by plants and reuse them. They also eliminate carbon dioxide through respiration.

3 When a carnivore eats a herbivore, it reuses carbon by incorporating this compound into its body. Carnivores also eliminate carbon dioxide through respiration.

4 The decomposers release carbon dioxide into the atmosphere through respiration.

5 Factories and automobiles burn carbon deposited underground in the form of hydrocarbons and release it as carbon dioxide into the atmosphere.

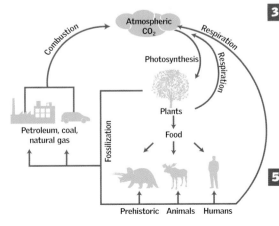

Combustion

Atmospheric CO_2

Respiration

Photosynthesis

Respiration

Plants

Food

Petroleum, coal, natural gas

Fossilization

Prehistoric | Animals | Humans

Of all organic material on Earth, 99% corresponds to plants and algae. The rest, in animals, does not exceed 1%.

TERTIARY CONSUMERS
These are the carnivores that eat other carnivores. Some food chains have as many as five trophic levels.

SECONDARY CONSUMERS
These consumers are the carnivores that feed on herbivores. Secondary consumers make use of a small part of the chemical energy stored in primary consumers.

100

species or more can form a food web within an ecosystem.

Not every ecosystem has the Sun as its principal source of energy. Once scientists were able to explore the great depths of the ocean, they began to discover ecosystems whose primary producers are bacteria that use the heat from the Earth's interior as their primary source of energy. These organisms live under extreme conditions, in dark habitats under very high pressures, with temperatures that can exceed 570° F (300° C).

The Biosphere

Only a small part of the Earth is inhabited by living things: the surface, the oceans, the first 5 miles (8 km) of the atmosphere above the ground, and the area beneath the ground as far as plant roots reach. The biosphere makes up this tiny portion of the planet. Studying the biosphere helps to reveal the patterns by which different forms of life became established and the parameters that affect the distribution of species and ecosystems. ●

The Living Portion of the Planet

■■ The distance from the center of the Earth to its surface is a little more than 3,700 miles (6,000 km). The biosphere, which contains all known living things, is a thin layer that does not exceed 12.5 miles (20 km) in thickness.

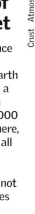
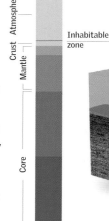

Atmosphere
Crust
Mantle
Core

Inhabitable zone

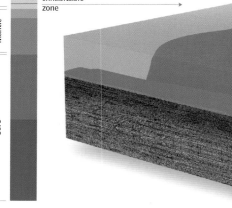

Diversity and Distribution

■■ The astonishing diversity of life and its distribution on the planet are determined by a variety of factors related to Earth's evolutionary history.

CONTINENTAL DRIFT

In the 1960s, scientists began to accept the theory of continental drift, which states that the shape and arrangement of the continents are not permanent. Since the breakup of a supercontinent called Pangaea about 200 million years ago, continental blocks have remained isolated from each other. Many forms of life on each continental block evolved independently of life on other blocks. This situation resulted in an increase in biodiversity.

1.2 inches (3 cm)

The distance that the continents move every year. Incidentally, this is also the approximate speed at which fingernails grow.

Permian
(270 million years ago)

The continents are joined together in Pangaea. At the end of this period, the greatest mass extinction in history occurs and almost wipes out life on the planet.

Triassic
(215 million years ago)

The dinosaurs appear. About 200 million years ago, Pangaea begins to divide into two supercontinents: Laurasia and Gondwana.

Jurassic
(180 million years ago)

Gondwana begins to break up, producing a period of tremendous earthquakes and volcanic eruptions. Dinosaurs are the dominant form of animal life. This is the time of the great herbivorous saurians.

Cretaceous
(65 million years ago)

The breakup of Gondwana continues, and Laurasia begins to fragment. India is about to collide with Asia, which will create the Himalaya Mountains. Flowering plants appear. At the end of this period, the dinosaurs become extinct.

The World Today

After the breakup, some continents, such as North and South America, become joined once again. This initiates an exchange of fauna and flora. Continental masses continue to move.

Pangaea

Laurasia

Gondwana

10,000 years

The period of time since the last Ice Age, when glaciers advanced across Europe and North America and the sea level fell.

620 miles (1,000 km)

The greatest width of the Gulf Stream.
(It can reach a depth of 330 feet [100 meters].)

Tectonic Processes

As they move, the continents can collide with one another and, in the process, produce significant changes in the landscape. Populations of living things can become divided, and their fragments may evolve independently from one another. Changes in the climate also alter life-forms.

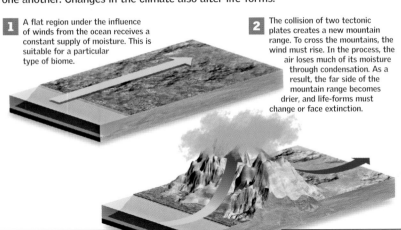

1 A flat region under the influence of winds from the ocean receives a constant supply of moisture. This is suitable for a particular type of biome.

2 The collision of two tectonic plates creates a new mountain range. To cross the mountains, the wind must rise. In the process, the air loses much of its moisture through condensation. As a result, the far side of the mountain range becomes drier, and life-forms must change or face extinction.

Natural Catastrophes

Intense volcanic eruptions, asteroid collisions with the Earth's surface, large earthquakes, and tsunamis have been major influences on life throughout the history of the Earth. At times, these events have produced mass extinctions.

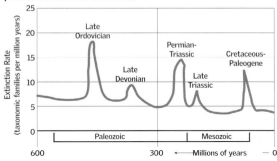

Paleontologists have identified five mass extinctions during the course of the Earth's evolutionary history. The extinction of the dinosaurs at the end of the Cretaceous (65 million years ago) was one of the most important. This mass extinction is also the most investigated.

Ocean Currents

The circulation of ocean waters is another important factor that affects climate and thus the distribution of species.

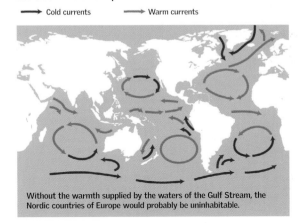

Without the warmth supplied by the waters of the Gulf Stream, the Nordic countries of Europe would probably be uninhabitable.

Changes in Climate

The Earth's climate undergoes constant change, alternating between periods that are warm and wet and periods that are cool.

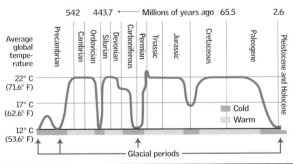

Biodiversity

Contemplating tropical rainforests and coral reefs can be wonderful. At the same time, however, it can be overwhelming because of the abundance and variety of organisms that live in these environments. There are strong indications that the greater the variety of species in an ecosystem, the greater the capacity of the ecosystem to adjust to environmental changes that could potentially threaten it. In addition, research suggests that ecosystems with poor biodiversity are more vulnerable to external factors (such as climate change and invasive species). These observations serve as a wake-up call to human beings, whose activities have disturbed and reduced the biodiversity of the planet. ●

An Atlas of Variety

It still is not possible to determine how many species inhabit the Earth. What is known is that biodiversity is greatest at or near the tropics. Biodiversity tends to decrease as one approaches the poles.

This map, made at Bonn University, Germany, shows indexes of biodiversity for vascular plants—that is, the majority of the plant kingdom. Some plants (such as algae, mosses, liverworts), however, are not included here.

Species, Genes, and Ecosystems

The concept of biodiversity is typically used to refer to the abundance of species, but it has other meanings in other fields of ecology.

Genetic Diversity
The genetic characteristics of small, isolated populations in which only a few individuals interbreed are poor when compared to those with larger and more diverse populations. The lack of genetic variability makes a population more susceptible to external changes.

Purebred dogs tend to be more "delicate" than most mutts because they are the product of breeding by members of a population with low genetic variability.

The Diversity of Species
About 1.5 million species have been described, but the total number of species of living things on the planet is uncertain. As many as 10 million or 100 million species are thought to exist. In addition, it is thought that ecosystems with greater biodiversity are less susceptible to environmental changes than ecosystems with lower biodiversity. In the long run, diverse ecosystems have a higher capacity for recuperation.

The Diversity of Ecosystems
The biosphere is made up of a great number of ecosystems. This diversity gives the biosphere stability and balance and makes it more resilient to major changes. The loss of ecosystems weakens the biosphere and makes it more vulnerable.

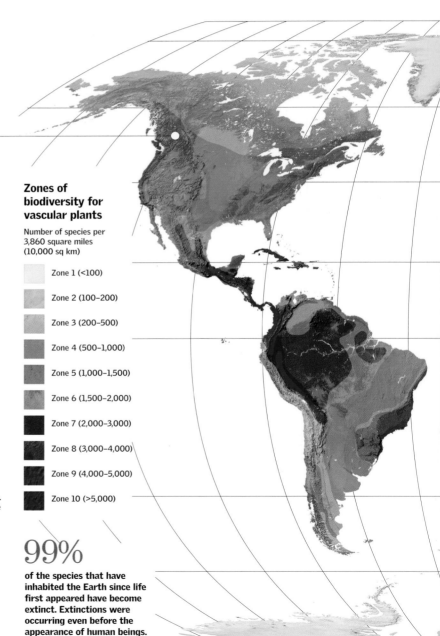

Zones of biodiversity for vascular plants

Number of species per 3,860 square miles (10,000 sq km)

- Zone 1 (<100)
- Zone 2 (100–200)
- Zone 3 (200–500)
- Zone 4 (500–1,000)
- Zone 5 (1,000–1,500)
- Zone 6 (1,500–2,000)
- Zone 7 (2,000–3,000)
- Zone 8 (3,000–4,000)
- Zone 9 (4,000–5,000)
- Zone 10 (>5,000)

99%
of the species that have inhabited the Earth since life first appeared have become extinct. Extinctions were occurring even before the appearance of human beings.

Balanced

Although it is still the subject of heated debate, an increasing number of ecologists maintain that systems with greater diversity are more stable and balanced than those with a meager variety of species.

◄ The diagram at left shows an ecosystem of considerable biodiversity with complex food webs.

The ecosystem at right is similar. It is, however, more limited in the sense that its food webs are simpler. The species in this ecosystem have become more vulnerable because they need to depend on fewer resources to survive. In some cases, species depend on a single resource. ►

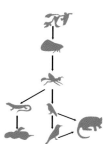

The Loss of Biodiversity

Human activity is one of the principal factors in the loss of biodiversity today, although it is a process that is difficult to measure.

The chart indicates how different factors that are the result of human activity in specific environments affect biodiversity. The present-day trends of these impacts are also shown.

Environment		Change of habitat	Climate change	Over-exploitation	Pollution
Forest	Boreal	↗	↑	→	↑
	Temperate	↘	↑	→	↑
	Tropical	↑	↑	↗	↑
Coastal		↗	↑	↗	↑
Rivers, lakes, and ponds		↑	↑	→	↑

Impact during the 20th century

- Low
- Moderate
- High
- Very high

Current Tendency

- ↘ Decreasing
- → Ongoing
- ↗ Increasing
- ↑ Rapidly increasing

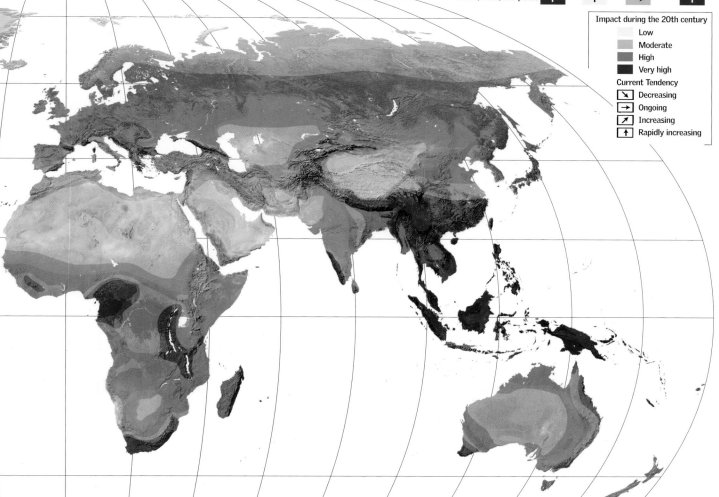

Keystone Species

Some species at the top of the trophic chain are considered "keystone species" because of the effect the loss of this species would have on an ecosystem's biodiversity. One experiment demonstrates that after the elimination of the starfish *Pisaster* in an area inhabited by 15 species, diversity fell to 8 species. This decrease in biodiversity occurred because a dominant species of mussels was allowed to establish itself. These mussels were formerly kept under control by the starfish. *Pisaster* fed on the mussels' prey and therefore left the mussel with limited resources. When the starfish disappeared, the mussel population could freely use these resources. The population of mussels grew, and mussel species outcompeted others.

Pisaster starfish eating a mussel.

Major Biomes of the World

Earth's land areas can be categorized according to the characteristics of the vegetation that they support. These regions of vegetation are repeated on different continents, and their existence depends in good measure on the occurrence of similar climates, soils, and geography. These regions are known as biomes. For a given biome that spans two regions of the

GREEN PARADISE
The Danum Valley in Malaysia acts like a large green lung that pumps oxygen into the air and creates a relaxing atmosphere.

world, equivalent species of animals and microorganisms may occur. Even though they are not related genetically, equivalent organisms have evolved comparable forms as the result of adopting similar strategies in their quest to adapt to the environment. Ecology includes the study of biomes and the ways energy and matter move through its member species as a means of learning about the workings of life. ●

Habitats of the World

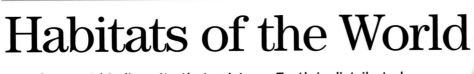

T he great biodiversity that exists on Earth is distributed among specific habitats, the climatic and geologic conditions of which produce specific types of soil, which in turn determine the area's flora and fauna. A biome is a large habitat region that is defined by a characteristic grouping of organisms together with the surrounding environment. Biomes can occur on land or in water. ●

The Climate Factor

Without a doubt, climate is the most important factor in the distribution of habitats. Such elements as wind, temperature, and precipitation govern the properties of the soil, and therefore the growth of plants, which forms the basis of all biomes. Moisture-laden winds intercepted by mountain ranges produce rainy areas with exuberant forests on one side of the range and arid conditions on the other. Tropical temperatures are a determining factor in the development of coral reefs. Pronounced low winter temperatures can result in the complete loss of tall flora from a habitat, as occurs in the tundra that surrounds the Arctic. The effects of climate, at times beneficial and at other times harmful, drive the complex and varied adaptations of organisms. Some animals have acquired specialized anatomies, whereas others migrate to areas with better conditions.

THE DISTRIBUTION OF HABITATS Communities of organisms are not distributed arbitrarily. The principal determining factors are air temperature and the availability of water. Temperature decreases with an increase in latitude, and water changes from a liquid to a solid in cold environments. These factors strongly affect the presence of plants and animals and produce very diverse habitats that range from lush tropical rainforests to stark polar and tundra habitats.

NORTHERN HEMISPHERE

SUNLIGHT

SOUTHERN HEMISPHERE

SEASONAL CHANGES
The 23.5° inclination of the Earth's axis, in combination with the Earth's revolution around the Sun, causes the seasonal variation of sunlight in the Northern and Southern Hemispheres.

ARCTIC 1 TUNDRA

SUBARCTIC 2 TAIGA

TEMPERATE 3

DESERT STEPPE GRASSLAND FOREST

TROPICAL 4

SAVANNA RAINFOREST

DESERT

0 150 250 500 1,000 2,000 4,000 8,000

AVERAGE ANNUAL PRECIPITATION (IN MM; 100 MM IS ABOUT 4 INCHES)

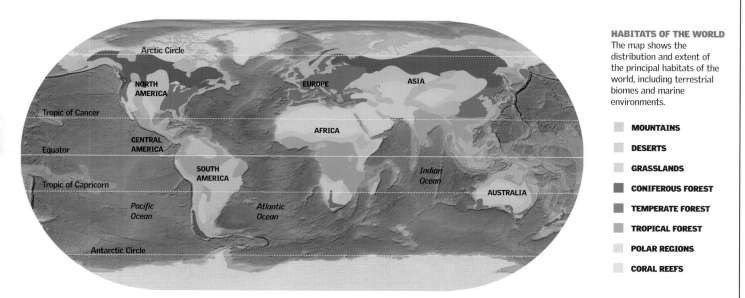

HABITATS OF THE WORLD
The map shows the distribution and extent of the principal habitats of the world, including terrestrial biomes and marine environments.

◻ **MOUNTAINS**

◻ **DESERTS**

◻ **GRASSLANDS**

◼ **CONIFEROUS FOREST**

◼ **TEMPERATE FOREST**

◻ **TROPICAL FOREST**

◻ **POLAR REGIONS**

◻ **CORAL REEFS**

Biodiversity

Every environment has particular characteristics that affect the species that inhabit it. Climate, geology, and other species in the area create a set of conditions that drive the selection of adaptations. These adaptations will determine whether a given species will survive in a given habitat. Skin covered with spines, warm coats of fur, and colorful markings are some of the traits that animals have acquired through the process of natural selection. These traits help species defend themselves against predators, protect themselves from unfavorable climates, or find mates. Among many other specific examples, algae called zoochlorellas live inside the bodies of certain corals and other animals in a mutually beneficial association. In addition, birds such as the oxpecker eat the mites that live on the skin of the water buffalo and other large mammals.

DESERTS
The moloch (*Moloch horridus*), a lizard from Australia, has an armor of sharp, thornlike spines that covers even its head. The protection provided by the spines is essential for this species. The moloch stays in one place for an extended time to feed on ants.

POLAR REGIONS
A thick white coat covers the polar bear (*Ursus maritimus*) and protects it from the extremely cold temperatures of the Arctic. Despite this adaptation, the polar bear is inactive in the winter. It hibernates in a den and survives on its large reserves of body fat.

CORAL REEFS
The spotted clown fish (*Amphiprion* species) lives in the tropical Pacific in association with a sea anemone that allows it to feed and rest among its tentacles. The fish receives protection. It repays this service by keeping the anemone clean. Because both species benefit from this relationship, the interaction is one of mutualism.

TROPICAL FORESTS
As a form of protection, many frogs secrete toxins that can cause paralysis and even death. Brilliant colors are often an indication of the strength of their poison. Such signals allow these frogs to make their way through a forest without being bothered by potential predators. Coloration that serves as a warning is said to be aposematic.

Species Counts

Near the Equator, the Sun passes high overhead all year round, which results in consistently high temperatures. Together with high rainfall, constant high temperatures create the optimum climatic conditions for life. Tropical rainforests are places with the highest concentration of species. The number of species progressively decreases away from the tropics. At the polar ice caps, the lack of biodiversity is compensated for by the large size of animal populations.

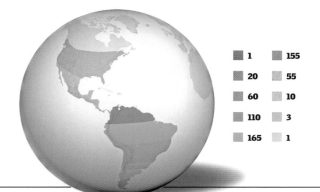

◻ 1 　 ◻ 155

◻ 20 　 ◻ 55

◻ 60 　 ◻ 10

◻ 110 　 ◻ 3

◻ 165 　 ◻ 1

TROPICAL HUMMINGBIRDS
Hummingbirds are a group of birds native to the Western Hemisphere. The high temperatures and humidity in tropical rainforests foster the vast diversity of these birds. About 150 species of hummingbirds live in Ecuador.

Land Biomes

The different temperatures and moisture levels that affect the earth's surface determine the aptness of soils, which serve as the foundation for sustaining habitats. They also have direct impact on the variety of their animal and plant species, and, therefore, on their ability to adapt in order to survive. The biomes located on solid ground are grouped primarily into forests (temperate, coniferous, and tropical), grasslands, mountains, deserts, and polar regions. ●

The Soil

The soil is the foundation of life on Earth. Here, plants extract the mineral nutrients and water from which to grow. Soil is formed by the interactions between rock and the atmosphere, water, and living things. The resulting alteration of the minerals in the bedrock creates an overlying layer of material from which the plants of the various biomes can grow. The various climatic and biological conditions present in a given habitat produce a unique type of soil. Soil itself varies in accordance with the composition of its layers, yielding a distinct mixture of mineral and organic matter.

HUMUS

A HORIZON

B HORIZON

C HORIZON

R HORIZON

STRATA
The soil is a key factor in the establishment of each biome. The proportion and composition of the soil's horizons, or layers, directly affects plant growth.
The types of plants present in the biome determine the fauna that will live in the biome. Although some soils exhibit every standard horizon, others are made up of only a few.
For example, the top layer of humus characteristic of grassland soils is absent in desert regions. In deserts, soil is usually crusted with calcium salts.

Animal Demographics

The distribution of wild animals into distinct populations can occur as the result of natural obstacles or fences and other human-made barriers that cross the land that the animals occupy. A population consists of a group of animals of the same species that interact and occupy a specific place.

The characteristic traits of a population are its size, birth rate, death rate, age distribution, and spatial distribution. Two or more species can share the same habitat without competing with each other if their environmental niches do not overlap. This is the case with grazing animals on the savanna.

COOPERATION
The animals grazing on the African savanna do not compete with one another. They complement each other to benefit the plants, which are specially adapted for intense grazing and fires.

GERENUK eats the leaves up to 10 feet (3 meters) from the ground

GIRAFFE takes advantage of its peculiar anatomy to reach the leaves and new shoots of tall acacias

ZEBRA looks for the high, tender shoots of grasses

GNU feeds on grass leaves and seed pods

DIK-DIKS eat the leaves of shrubs that are no higher than 5 feet (1.5 meters).

GAZELLES AND TOPIS consume the short, dry stalks that are left by the other animals.

Forest Layers

Forest biomes are divided vertically into a number of variable levels, or layers. The principal levels of a temperate forest are the herbaceous, shrub, and tree layers. In a tropical forest, the corresponding layers are the forest floor, the understory, and the canopy. Tropical forests also have an upper level called the emergent layer, which can reach a height of 245 feet (75 meters). There are characteristic flora and fauna for each level. One of the primary factors driving the development of forests is competition for light. This competition manifests itself in the tropical forest canopy by the presence of lianas and epiphytes. At the ground level there is little light, and the vegetative cover is made up of dead leaves and fallen branches. The biomass of this decaying material is equivalent to the biomass that plants of the forest produce in one year. Other organisms, such as fungi and parasitic plants, typically grow under these conditions.

DECIDUOUS FOREST
Trees in this temperate forest lose their leaves in the winter and leaf again in the spring.
CLIMATE The average annual temperature varies between 75° F and 88° F (24 and 31° C), depending on the altitude, and the relative humidity ranges from 60% to 80%.
SOIL It is a thick, rich layer of decaying matter that harbors invertebrates and other organisms.
VEGETATION The hundreds of tree species are veritable living power plants.

Extreme Regions

Climatic factors such as extreme cold and a scarcity of water from precipitation create habitats in which the conditions for life lead to poor vegetation. This lack of high-quality vegetation keeps animal life from becoming established. In the polar regions, the low temperatures reduce the variety of animal species without diminishing their numbers. On the other hand, the water deficit in deserts requires specialized adaptive mechanisms (such as the water-storage capability of cacti). Often, these specialized plants have spines to help increase the efficiency of water conservation.

THE ARCTIC AND TUNDRA

In places where the climate is too cold and the winters too long, the coniferous forest of the Northern Hemisphere gives way to tundra, a vast treeless region that surrounds the Arctic.

CLIMATE Strong winds reach speeds of 30 to 60 miles (48–96 km) per hour, while the average annual temperature is 7° F (–14° C).

SOIL Except for places where animals have left droppings, the soil is poor in nutrients and minerals.

VEGETATION The few species include grasses, mosses, lichens, and sparse shrubs.

DESERT

A desert forms in areas where the evaporation of water exceeds the rainfall.

CLIMATE Low precipitation—less than 6 inches (about 150 mm) annually. The temperature range is large, as great as 55° F (about 30° C) between night and day.

SOIL Poorly developed. It has little organic matter in its top layer.

VEGETATION Notable plants include cacti, which have developed systems for storing water and networks of deep roots to capture water from intermittent rains.

EROSION

Wind, rain, and chemical processes tend to erode the desert plateaus, creating a variety of shapes including deep ravines, isolated hills, arches, and river gullies.

Permafrost

The ground in the tundra has underground layers that can remain frozen for more than two years. In the coldest areas, the extent of the permafrost is continuous. It can vary from discontinuous to sporadic in regions where the average temperature is just below 32° F (0° C). The organic matter at the surface gives off greenhouse gases when it thaws.

CONTINUOUS   SPORADIC
DISCONTINUOUS   ISOLATED

Forests

The high density and growth rate of trees—where there is the right amount of light and moisture—give rise to several types of forests in which a complex biological community is adapted to the prevailing temperatures. Depending on the region, a forest may be temperate, boreal, or tropical. Temperate forests are located mainly in the Northern Hemisphere, and tropical forests are located near the Equator. Boreal forests are located below the tundra and are Earth's youngest biome. The trees in temperate forests may be either evergreen or deciduous.

CONIFEROUS OR BOREAL FOREST

Conifers—trees that reproduce by means of cones—can withstand winter snows, and they form thick, protective forests.

CLIMATE In the winter, the temperature commonly is –13° F (–25° C), but sometimes reaches –49° F (–45° C).

SOIL It is acidic as the result of a thick covering of dead tree needles.

VEGETATION It is limited because of soil acidity and the lack of light that penetrates to the ground.

TROPICAL FOREST

Located near the Equator, tropical forests grow constantly and have a great variety of species.

CLIMATE It is warm and humid all year round.

SOIL Foliage that falls on the ground forms a layer of putrefying plant matter, which is rapidly mineralized by the conditions. The predominant types of soils, called oxisols, have a characteristic red color because of the presence of iron and aluminum oxides.

VEGETATION It has the greatest variety of trees, which typically have slender trunks. The forest canopy can reach a height of 245 feet (75 meters). The leaves in the canopy shelter the fauna in the forest below. Only a few palms can grow in the shade of the forest floor.

Grassland

In both temperate and tropical climates, there are great open expanses covered with grasses. They create an ideal habitat for herbivores such as bison and rodents. The stalks of grass growing from ground level are adapted to animal grazing. The presence of fast-running predators, the lack of hiding places, and the risk of drought and fires, however, make grasslands a challenging environment in which to survive. ●

Temperate Grassland

Before the arrival of agriculture, the grasslands of the Northern Hemisphere were covered with endless prairies. Far from the moderating influence of the oceans, these areas experience hot summers and long, cold winters. Curiously, in contrast with the prolific leaves typical of plants in other biomes, grassland plants have prolific roots. The roots help store nutrients in case of drought or fire. In addition to being a rich source of food, the roots keep the soil firm. The firm soil allows rodents to develop an extensive network of underground burrows.

EMU *Dromaius novaehollandiae*
This large bird—the largest in Australia—can grow to a height of 6.5 feet (2 meters). Its feet have three toes that are adapted for running. Although it has lost the ability to fly, it is a fast runner and swimmer. It is covered with a fleecy plumage that insulates it from the Sun's rays. After the chicks hatch from their eggs, the male emu cares for them until they reach eight months of age.

BLACK-TAILED PRAIRIE DOG
Cynomys ludovicianus
This rodent, which makes its home in grasslands, emits a howl similar to that of a dog. It is a social animal, and it is known for the interconnected burrows that it digs. Prairie dogs also form subgroups for protection from predators.

Winner in Speed

Given the presence of very fast predators, running is a good means of escape for prey. Many mammals can run fast, but certain birds that do not fly (ostriches, emus, and ñandus) can, too—at speeds up to 45 miles (about 70 km) per hour. These flightless birds can maintain this speed for 30 minutes! The birds also make use of their height and large eyes to spot possible predators from long distances away. In contrast, slower prey animals often seek refuge in burrows.

125 miles (200 km)

the distance kangaroos sometimes travel in search of water during the dry season

RED KANGAROO
Macropus rufus
This animal is the largest living marsupial. It uses its highly developed sense of smell to find water. In addition, it has a heavy tail that it uses as a pendulum. Together with its energy-storing tendons, the red kangaroo can spring forward when it runs. When red kangaroos play or fight among themselves, they can stand on their hind feet and either kick or act as if they are boxing. Young kangaroos are born at a relatively early stage of development. They are nourished through one of the mother's teats inside a protective pouch. The baby kangaroo does not leave the pouch permanently until some 200 days later.

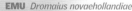

Savanna

In the tropical climates of the Southern Hemisphere, grasslands are characterized by a landscape made up of a few scattered trees (such as the African acacia, a key source of food). Grazing elephants help the acacia to distribute its seeds. Eaten seeds appear in the dung of elephants. Some animals, however, hinder the acacia's growth by nibbling on its shoots before they can develop. Many trees on the savanna have an umbrella-like shape, as a result of the "trim" they receive from giraffes. The savanna is hot all year round, in contrast to the temperate grassland, and its rainy season is followed by a long dry season. During this time, many animals need to travel long distances to find food and water.

AFRICAN ELEPHANT
Loxodonta africana
The male elephant is the largest living land animal. It lives for about 60 years. Its trunk has two prolongations that are used for picking up objects. One function of its curving tusks is to dig up the soil to extract the extra salt that it needs for its diet.

Life in Herds

The landscape of a grassland provides few hiding places, and many animals opt to live in a herd to reduce the chances of becoming injured in attacks by predators. Some animals of the herd feed, while others remain alert. In the 19th century, herds of gazelles in southern Africa gathered together in numbers of more than 10 million, a number comparable to the size of the bison herds that once roamed the North American prairie. Because an individual's risk of separation from the herd is high, many species have glands in their hooves that produce an odorous substance. This substance will lead the lost member back to the herd.

Cellulose

Grass contains large amounts of cellulose, a carbohydrate that is difficult to digest. Some animals, such as the giraffe, are able to break it down with the help of enzymes produced by their stomach bacteria.

GIRAFFE
Giraffa camelopardalis
The giraffe's unique anatomy allows for it to graze the leaves of trees almost 20 feet (6 meters) high. Despite its long neck, the giraffe, like other mammals, has seven cervical vertebrae. It uses its long tongue, which can extend some 18 inches (45 cm), to reach acacia branches, while its lobulated teeth rake off the leaves. There are regional variations in the pattern of its spotted skin, and these patterns are useful in the identification of the nine subspecies, including the reticulated giraffe. The males establish a dominance hierarchy by striking each other with their necks. Giraffe skulls are reinforced with an extra bone.

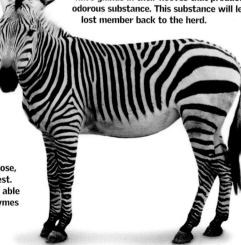

BURCHELL'S ZEBRA *Equus burchelli*
This animal has a wide field of vision and acute hearing. Its stripes provide camouflage; however, it is thought that they may also regulate temperature or serve a social function that helps individual animals recognize each other. To help verify the odor given off by females when they are ready to mate, the male enhances the sensitivity of his sense of smell by lifting his upper lip.

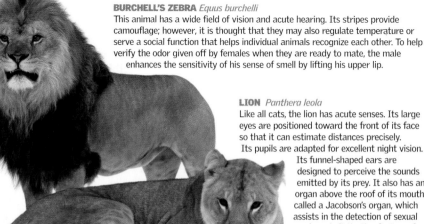

LION *Panthera leola*
Like all cats, the lion has acute senses. Its large eyes are positioned toward the front of its face so that it can estimate distances precisely. Its pupils are adapted for excellent night vision. Its funnel-shaped ears are designed to perceive the sounds emitted by its prey. It also has an organ above the roof of its mouth, called a Jacobson's organ, which assists in the detection of sexual odors. A distinctive feature of male lions is a thick mane. The mane makes males appear larger.

African Savanna

The most extensive savanna in the world lies in Africa. In contrast with the North American prairie, the grassy areas of the savanna are mixed with a few shrubs and trees, such as acacias and baobabs. The herbivores that feed on them (such as giraffes, rhinoceroses, antelope, and elephants) avoid the competition for food by eating at different levels. The alternation between wet and dry seasons brings about astonishing migrations of animals that raise large clouds of dust in their passage. ●

LEVELS OF TREE GRAZING

Although many animals survive by feeding on the sea of grasses that grow on the savannah, other animals seek nourishment from the savanna's scattered trees. Different species of animals eat from branches at different heights. Whereas the rhinoceros and dik-dik eat from the lowest branches, elephants and giraffes, thanks to their higher reach, can eat from the higher branches of the tree. Giraffes can consume leaves off branches as high as about 16 feet (5 meters) off the ground.

GIRAFFE
Giraffa camelopardalis

AFRICAN ELEPHANT
Loxodonta africana

MARABOU
Leptoptilos crumeniferus

BURCHELL'S ZEBRA
Equus burchelli

AFRICAN WHITE-BACKED VULTURE
Gyps africanus

WILDEBEEST
Connochaetes Taurinus

Herbivores and Predators

The abundance of grasses and other plants in the savanna leads to the presence of a great variety of animals that graze on them. While zebras and buffalos feed on the tallest shoots, gnus and gazelles graze on the lower leafy layers. Ruminants (such as the antelope, buffalo, and giraffe) have microorganisms in their digestive tracts that decompose the cellulose of grass. The herbivorous inhabitants of the savanna serve as food for predators (such as the lion, leopard, and hyena). A notable predator is the cheetah, which is known for its rapid sprints. Other animals on the savanna include carrion-eaters, such as various species of eagles and vultures that fly in circles to locate the bodies of dead animals.

TERMITE
Isoptera

Social insects, termites live in immense colonies. Termites take dead plant matter to their nests, where they cultivate the fungi on which they feed. They can digest wood with the help of microorganisms that live in their intestines.

Termite Mounds

These incredible hills, which take termites between 10 and 50 years to build, serve as protection from predators and the hot climate. The termite colony begins with a chamber about 12 inches (30 cm) deep, a location in which the king and queen mate. The termites that hatch from the eggs are charged with constructing the mound. Walls built from bits of wood are mixed with excrement to form irregular, arched rooms. A sophisticated system of tunnels and chimneys provides ventilation and cooling.

TERMITE MOUNDS

ACACIA
African species are the source of gum arabic and gum senegal, which is used to cure skins. The wood of the acacia is strong, heavy, and dense. It is used commercially.

SCATTERED TREES
Unlike temperate grasslands, which are completely open lands, savannas have a mixture of grassy areas and scattered shrubs and trees. Growth is limited both by the region's precipitation and by the type of soil that is present. The hard layers of the soil block the penetration of roots. The growth of the trees is also controlled by the depth of the water table, and the proximity of surface water is also important.

SPEED
The cheetah can accelerate to 60 miles (about 100 km) per hour in just five seconds.

ILLEGAL HUNTING
Only about 7,000 rhinoceroses remain. The animal is pursued by hunters for its horn, which has a purported medicinal value.

Herds
Most of the herbivorous animals on the savanna live in herds to protect themselves against predators such as lions, cheetahs, and wild dogs. Herds of zebras can contain as many as 200,000 individuals, whereas herds of wildebeest, or gnus, can reach 1.5 million in size. In May, with the arrival of the dry season, wildebeest herds migrate in search of food and water from Africa's southern grasslands to the east and north. When the rains begin and grasses begin to grow again, the herds return. They can cover distances as great as 1,500 miles (2,500 km) in one year.

WHITE RHINOCEROS
Ceratotherium simum

LION
Panthera leo

COEXISTENCE
The stems of grasses as well as other plants sprout from the ground's surface. In some species, plants begin well below ground. As a result, most plants are not destroyed by the animals that graze on them.

DUNG BEETLE
Scarabaeidae
This beetle uses the dung produced by the savanna's large mammals. It forms the dung into balls into which it deposits its eggs. The beetle buries the dung ball, and its larva later feed on it.

Desert

Life in the desert must adapt to very adverse conditions. Deserts are very dry because of scant precipitation; however, they are also subjected to daytime heat, strong winds, and large temperature swings between day and night. Desert animals live according to a rigorous "water economy"; they collect water wherever possible and minimize its loss. Most desert organisms recycle food by consuming their excrement to recover water. Some can even store extra water within their bodies for later use. ●

The Desert

Deserts are typically located within the tropics, in regions with sustained high air pressure. Daytime surface temperatures can reach 160° F (70° C), and true deserts have less than 5.9 inches (15 cm) of precipitation annually. What little vegetation is present is mainly made up of cacti and other succulents. These plants carry out a unique form of photosynthesis that is specially adapted to desert conditions; these plants open their stomas to absorb carbon dioxide only at night. The lack of plants seriously limits animal life in this environment. The most important deserts in the world include the Sahara and Kalahari of Africa, the Arabian and Gobi deserts of Asia, and the deserts of western North America and Australia.

ARABIAN CAMEL OR DROMEDARY
Camelus dromedarius
Among this camel's many adaptations is its hump, which it uses to store water. It can raise its body temperature and reduce perspiration to conserve moisture in the intense heat of the desert.

MOLOCH OR THORNY DEVIL
Moloch horridus
Difficult to spot because of its camouflage, this lizard can take in water through its skin, where capillary action carries it to its mouth. The armor of thorny spines that covers its body protects it from attack. It is especially useful when it stays in one place for an extended period to feed.

Moving across Sand

The sand in the desert can be truly difficult for animals to move across. Heavy animals sink into it, whereas small animals struggle to get up and down the steep slopes of sliding sand. Camels and geckos have large feet that spread the body's weight out over the sand for stability. The horned viper travels across the sand by pushing itself forward off the ground. It creates tracks in the form of a "J."

WESTERN DIAMONDBACK RATTLESNAKE
Crotalus atrox
The most dangerous snake in the United States. It attacks with fangs, which contain a potent venom of toxins that can kill in minutes. It may shake the rattle on the tip of its tail as a warning.

The Semidesert

Compared to a true desert, a semidesert has more rainfall (up to 16 inches [40 cm] annually). Therefore, it is a more productive environment. Plants that create thick tangles of roots form important ground cover. In addition, there are species of trees with sharp protective spines designed to funnel water to their buried roots. In contrast, the cactus directs water to its stalks and leaves. Also present are caterpillars that produce a poisonous secretion; only a few animals eat them for food. Many semideserts are hot all year, whereas others are very cold in the winter. In the desert regions of the Rocky Mountains, some species hibernate through the winter because of the cold temperatures.

BLACK-TAILED JACKRABBIT
Lepus californicus

This animal has large, thin ears that can detect even the slightest sound. The ears have several capillaries that carry blood near the surface of the skin. This arrangement helps the animal release heat to maintain body temperature. The black-tailed jackrabbit can hop quickly, reaching a speed of 35 miles (56 km) per hour. It lives alone and associates with other individuals only during mating season, when it engages in chasing, fighting, and ceremonial jumping. It ingests most of its food twice to maximize the amount of nutrients received. Poaching has reduced its numbers, especially in some areas of Mexico and the United States.

CLARETCUP HEDGEHOG
Echinocereus triglochidiatus

This cactus gets its name because its shape resembles that of hedgehog. It is also known as a "claret cup," because of its cup-shaped flowers, which remain open for three to five days. Its red fruit are edible.

Like other cacti, it has a thick covering enclosed in spines. The spines keep animals away and shade the plant's surface to reduce the loss of moisture. This plant stores water in the pulp of its fleshy stalks.

Conservation of Water

Every organism that lives in the desert needs to make sure that it has an adequate amount of water. Desert animals, unlike those of other habitats, lose very little water from their droppings, urine, and respiration or through their skin. Some animals gather to drink water from an oasis, whereas others eat foods rich in water. Some animals may also obtain water through the chemical reactions involved in metabolizing the food they eat. Certain rodents, for example, are very efficient at metabolizing water from seeds. On the other hand, species such as the camel do not become dehydrated easily.

COYOTE
Canis latrans

This fast runner, related to the domestic dog, lives only in North and Central America. Its characteristic nocturnal howling can either announce its location or mark its territory.

GILA MONSTER
Heloderma suspectum

This reptile, one of the largest poisonous lizards, moves slowly and makes use of its well-developed sense of smell to find and trap young rodents, birds, and insects. It bites its prey with sharp pointed teeth and injects venom produced by glands in its lower jaw. The bite is painful but not fatal to adult humans. The long tail contains fat, like the hump of a camel. The contrasting coloration of the skin can serve as camouflage or as a warning of the threat it poses to potential aggressors.

Semidesert

The modest rainfall that distinguishes this habitat from a true desert allows the growth of cacti, shrubs, and ephemeral plants. These plants manage in their short life spans to produce food that feeds local animals. The available food spurs the development of a wider range of fauna. Semideserts with cold winters, however, still present challenges to animals. They need to discover ways to store water and find refuge from the low temperatures. ●

RED-TAILED HAWK
Buteo jamaicensis

ELF OWL
Micrathene whitneyi

GILA WOODPECKER
Melanerpes uropygialis

KIT FOX
Vulpes macrotis

MINER'S CAT OR RINGTAIL
Bassariscus astutus

Living Without Water

Succulent plants store water from the area's scant precipitation in thick stems, fleshy leaves, and wide roots. These roots lie near the surface of the ground to maximize the plant's ability to absorb rainfall. An external cuticle regulates the evaporation of water. In the cactus, leaves appear as spines. This not only minimizes the loss of water but also protects the plant from thirsty animals. More than 90% of the weight of a cactus is water.

WOLF SPIDER
Lycosa tarentula

ARGENTINE ANT
Linepithema humile

ROADRUNNER
Geococcyx californianus
It can run about 20 miles (32 km) per hour when chasing prey.

WESTERN DIAMONDBACK
Crotalus atrox

INSECTS AND SPIDERS

The semidesert is home to numerous insects (such as fire ants, weevils, dragonflies, butterflies, and cicadas). Among the spiders of note are the tarantulas, which can hunt primarily by touch in darkness. The female black widow spider is known for the fact that it commonly kills the male. The venom of the black widow spider is stronger than that of a rattlesnake.

SAGUARO
Carnegiea gigantea
This cactus expands its external surfaces like an accordion to increase its water storage capacity, which can be as great as 2,400 gallons (9,000 liters). Its stem can grow to a height of 50 feet (15 meters), and its roots can penetrate down to a depth of 100 feet (30 meters).

The American Semidesert

Although a semidesert can be hot throughout the entire year, part of the American semidesert experiences severe winters; the temperature can fall as low as –22° F (–30° C). This region extends throughout the Sonoran and Mojave deserts in the United States. Insects become inactive, and many mammals hibernate. A few animals (such as bighorn sheep) use thick tangles of vegetation, woody plants, and cacti as sources of water and refuge from predators and the weather.

COYOTE
Canis latrans

WHITE-TAILED ANTELOPE SQUIRREL
Ammospermophilus leucurus

COLLARED PECCARY
Tayassu tajacu

BLACK-TAILED JACKRABBIT
Lepus californicus

CENTURY PLANT
Agave americana

DESERT TORTOISE
Gopherus agassizii

GILA MONSTER
Heloderma suspectum

SURVIVING WITHOUT WATER
Adult tortoises are able to survive almost a year without water. Their front legs are specially adapted to dig large, deep burrows, which they leave to find food in the morning and evening. They can live 50 to 80 years.

WIND SCORPION OR SUNSPIDER
Eremobates pallipes

NORTH AMERICAN BADGER
Taxidea taxus

SCORPION
For defense, the scorpion can inject poison from a stinger located at the end of its tail-shaped abdomen.

Protection

In order to escape the heat and avoid dehydration, some animals (such as the green frog, bull snake, trap-door spider, and kangaroo rat) excavate underground burrows or move into those built by other animals. Kangaroo rats seal the entrance to their hiding places to retain moisture. The trap-door spider uses the silk that it produces to cover the small pit into which it retreats.

Tropical Forest

Circling the Equator, where the high temperatures drive rapid rates of evaporation that result in copious rains, tropical rainforests constitute the biome with the greatest variety of species. The ecological importance of tropical rainforests is linked to their absorption of carbon dioxide. This biome acts as a stabilizing influence on the global climate, and its great aggregations of trees are veritable factories of oxygen that supply the entire planet. The trees also help maintain the water cycle and protect against floods and erosion. The plants of the rainforest are used for food, and ongoing scientific research continues to discover their potential pharmacological value. ●

Humid Tropical Forest

Unlike the tropical monsoon forest, in which precipitation falls only during the rainy season, the humid tropical forest receives precipitation all year long. Copious rainfall carries away silica and other substances from the soil, leaving it acidic and containing a high proportion of aluminum and iron oxides. These compounds give the soil a reddish or reddish-yellow color. Despite the poor soil, the warm, humid climate creates optimum conditions for life. Humid tropical forests have the greatest diversity of species, and these species interact in intense and complex ways. Certain mammals and other animals always move on the ground, but the great majority of animals move through the trees. Many animals rely on camouflage as a primary means of defense, and some are able to use mimicry. Most plant species are evergreens and have elliptical leaves. Some plants have leaves with points that allow water to drip away.

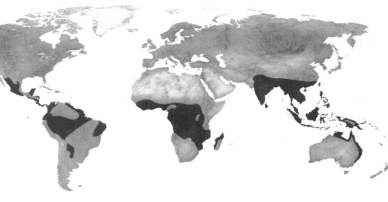

200

The number of tree species that can be found in just 2.5 acres (1 hectare) of a tropical rainforest.

UNDERSTORY
At this level, the trunks of the canopy trees are straight without branches. There are also shrubs and palms—such as rattan, lianas, and many climbing plants.

1 EMERGENT LAYER
Enormous isolated trees that can grow as high as 245 feet (75 meters). These trees, known as "emergents," serve as a refuge for nesting and an eating platform for animals.

2 CANOPY
This layer forms a continuous cover of branches and leafy foliage about 65 feet (20 meters) thick. The canopy occurs beneath the emergent layer. There are many fruits and flowers in the canopy.

3 UNDERSTORY
This layer is more open than the canopy, and it contains plants that are better adapted to life in the shadows. The buttresses formed by the roots of the canopy trees also occur at this level.

4 FLOOR
The little light that penetrates the dense foliage of the canopy produces a dark, calm environment with few plants.

LEVELS OF LIFE
The stable climate of the tropical forest, with its high temperature and humidity, causes some plants to focus their energy into growing very tall, whereas others adapt to the limited light of the forest floor. These different patterns of growth result in a forest with four well-defined layers, each with its own characteristic plant and animal species.

THE FOREST FLOOR
The leaves that constantly fall to the forest floor form a layer of decaying plant matter. This material is quickly consumed by insects and expelled as waste. This activity produces a rich source of nutrients for the roots of the trees.

At Ground Level

A thick layer of fallen leaves covers the lowest level of the tropical rainforest. The principal organisms found here are fungi and bacteria, which produce a fine layer of fertile earth called humus. The organic matter that falls to the ground decays rapidly from the humid conditions and regular rainfall. The trees spread a dense mat of roots out under the surface of the ground to obtain nutrients before they are washed away. Humans and large animals (such as jaguars, giant anteaters, gorillas, and deer) easily travel through this layer of the forest because the darkness at this level inhibits the growth of any dense vegetation. Tapirs and a few other mammals live on the forest floor. Tapirs eat fruit that falls from the canopy.

JAGUAR *Panthera onca*

The jaguar is an expert climber. When it is about to attack, it flattens its ears, dilates the pupils of its eyes, and shows its strong teeth in a display of aggression. Its skin coloration provides camouflage, and it keeps its sharp claws retracted until they are needed. The claws of the jaguar are extended by a mechanism similar to that of a switchblade.

59 inches (1,500 mm)

The minimum annual rainfall of a tropical rainforest. The rain acidifies the soil and washes some of it away.

COMMON BOA
Boa constrictor

This expert swimmer can hunt both in trees and at ground level. Its prey include birds and mammals, which are squeezed and suffocated by the boa's muscular coils. The colorful patterns on its body blur its outline and help it to remain camouflaged in its surroundings.

BUTTRESSES
Surprisingly, most of the ground beneath a tropical rainforest is made up of poor, infertile soils called oxisols. These soils, together with the lack of sunlight penetrating the forest canopy, hamper the growth of plants. The ground has an abundance of fungi, mosses, ferns, and enormous tree roots. These roots can build outward-oriented buttresses to support the weight of the largest trees.

2,500

The number of species of climbing plants and woody vines that grow from the forest floor. These species appear in the form of small shrubs that extend upward along tree trunks in search of light.

GOLIATH BIRD-EATING TARANTULA
Theraphosa blondi
It is the world's heaviest spider at 5.3 ounces (150 grams). It is the world's second-largest spider, measuring up to 11.8 inches (30 cm) across. Aggressive, voracious, and equipped with fangs and irritating hairs, this spider can even devour small snakes. The spider lives in deep burrows, and it produces a warning sound by rubbing parts of its body together.

ARMY ANTS
Eciton burchellii
In the forests of Central and South America, marauding army ants attract many types of birds. Birds rush to feed on the tiny animals that are flushed out of their hiding places in an attempt to flee the ants. This activity also draws other hunting species (such as lizards, toads, and parasitic flies).

GIANT ANTEATER
Myrmecophaga tridactyla

This anteater breaks open ant nests with the curved claws on its front feet. It then traps the ants with sticky saliva from its wormlike tongue. Its tongue can stretch to a length of 24 inches (60 cm).

SOUTH AMERICAN LOWLAND TAPIR
Tapirus terrestris
This streamlined tapir spends much of its time in water. It can swim to flee its predators. It has a short trunk that can be extended. The tapir depends on its well-developed sense of smell to find food and avoid danger.

PREHENSILE TRUNK
The tapir is able to use its extremely flexible trunk to detect smells at a distance. The trunk's prehensile organ is used for reaching high leaves and shoots.

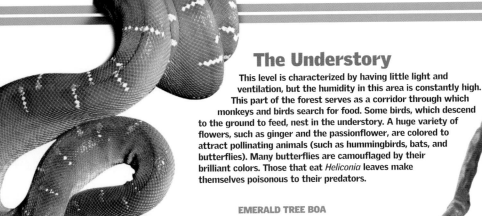

The Understory

This level is characterized by having little light and ventilation, but the humidity in this area is constantly high. This part of the forest serves as a corridor through which monkeys and birds search for food. Some birds, which descend to the ground to feed, nest in the understory. A huge variety of flowers, such as ginger and the passionflower, are colored to attract pollinating animals (such as hummingbirds, bats, and butterflies). Many butterflies are camouflaged by their brilliant colors. Those that eat *Heliconia* leaves make themselves poisonous to their predators.

WHITE-THROATED CAPUCHIN MONKEY
Cebus capucinus
This species is considered to be the smartest of the New World monkeys. It lives in groups of up to 20 members. When it leaves to search for insects, it repeats its call regularly to remain in contact with the group. The species is very territorial and marks its territory with urine. Although it finds some of its food on the forest floor, it gets most of it from the trees. It does, however, climb down from the trees to obtain water. This monkey can use its strong tail to hold onto tree branches and can climb very high into the trees. It also knows how to use rocks as tools to break open nuts and mollusks.

EMERALD TREE BOA
Corallus caninus
Its initial coloring is red, orange, or yellow. It does not acquire its characteristic intense green color until after its first year. Green coloration allows the snake to blend in with the green forest foliage and hide from birds of prey. The emerald tree boa has a strong, prehensile tail that it can firmly coil around tree branches. It can then hang with its head down as it waits to leap on and capture prey. This species has vertical pupils that help to detect movement.

TOCO TOUCAN
Ramphastos toco
Its large orange beak, which can extend up to 7 inches (19 cm), is used as a tool to reach food on the ends of branches. Its characteristic call is deep and husky.

360°

The circular range of motion of the gibbon's shoulder joint, an adaptation that allows it to move through the forest rapidly, swinging from branch to branch.

EPIPHYTIC PLANTS
These plants use the branches of the trees for support to reach sunlight. When it rains, they trap and collect so much water that the extra weight can cause the branch they sit on to break off.

1 RADIAL GROWTH
The leaves of bromeliads grow outward from the center of the plant.

2 POOL OF WATER
The leaves direct the rainwater into a small basinlike structure at the center of the plant.

3 VISITORS
Tadpoles, worms, mosquitoes, and crabs are some of the many animals that can be found in this central pool of water.

The Canopy

A vast supply of fruit, leaves, insects, and other sources of food is found in this layer. Consequently, many animals do not have to lower themselves to the ground to eat. The majority of forest fauna are present in the canopy, and travel through the branches has led to specialized adaptations, especially among certain species. Gibbons, for example, have prehensile hands and feet and long arms that can be used to swing from branch to branch (a form of locomotion called brachiation). Some birds, such as the quetzal, swallow fruit whole and regurgitate the pit. The pits can later sprout into a new plant. A large variety of plants called epiphytes climb and twist around tree branches to get closer to areas of sunlight.

4 CLINGING ROOTS
The bromeliad is firmly affixed to the branch of the tree by means of its roots, which provide plenty of support and stability even high above the ground.

Emergent Layer

The highest layer of the tropical forest has only a few very tall trees, up to 245 feet (75 meters) in height. Unlike the layers below it, the emergent layer is dry as a result of the intense sunlight. The leaves that form in this layer are tough. To minimize evaporation, leaves are small and coated in wax. The trees also make use of the strong winds that lash the crowns of the tree to disperse pollen and seeds. The emergent layer is also home to the harpy eagle, a strong and extraordinarily agile predator. The harpy eagle keeps watch on the canopy below for its prey.

OROPENDOLA NEST

The nest appears as a pendulum-shaped structure up to 1.6 feet (0.5 meters) in length, hung from high isolated trees. It is believed that the shape of the nest discourages predators, especially snakes. The nest is made of thin fibers and stems that are woven like a basket. An opening at the top serves as an entrance. The same tree may be used continuously by several generations of oropendolas as nesting sites. The nesting colonies are home to much activity, especially from January to May when the nests are being built or repaired. Oropendolas belong to the group of New World blackbirds. They are known by the loud, harsh gargling calls that they make.

LINNAEUS' TWO-TOED SLOTH
Choloepus didactylus

This tree-living species climbs to the ground to defecate. Its front legs are longer than its back legs, and it has two fingers with long, curved claws shaped like hooks. These hooks are ideal for its life in the trees. The sloth's long brown fur may have a greenish cast because algae may grow on it. The sloth's diet includes leaves. The sloth also plays an important part in the nutrient recycling process in the forest.

FRANQUET'S EPAULETTED BAT
Epomops franqueti

This winged mammal relies on its highly developed senses of hearing and smell. Because its vision is poor, it makes use of echolocation to orient itself in complete darkness. Feeding on fruit, it plays an important role in seed dispersal and thus the natural regeneration of the forest. It is one of three species of fruit bats in Africa that carry the Ebola virus.

3,000

The number of insects that an insectivorous bat typically eats in a single night. It finds the insects through echolocation. In this process, the bat produces sound waves, which return as echoes. The return speed of the echoes give the bat information about its environment.

SUN PARAKEET
Aratinga solstitialis

These peaceful and friendly parakeets are very social and live in groups with as many as 30 individuals. Their colors become brighter and more vivid as they age, which helps them blend into their surroundings and distract predators. In addition, they have a special ability to make and imitate sounds, which they use to attract attention. The parakeets can become aggressive when they are not able to carry on sociably. They also enjoy human company.

KING VULTURE
Sarcoramphus papa

Its wingspan can extend almost 6.6 feet (2 meters). It is named "king" because it is the largest vulture. It also scares away other vultures when it lands on a dead carcass. Its habits are difficult to study because it remains out of sight from observers at the top of trees or flies at great height. It does not migrate or build a nest. Instead, the king vulture uses other places, such as the crevices of trees, as its home.

ADAPTATION TO RAIN

Most rainforest trees have pointed leaves; this helps to draw off the water that falls on them.

MENELAUS BLUE MORPHO
Morpho menelaus

This iridescent butterfly drinks the juice of decomposing fruits. It draws in the juice through its proboscis, a tubular appendage that extends from its head. It also feeds on fungi and helps to spread their spores.

SCARLET MACAW
Ara macao

KING VULTURE
Sarcoramphus papa

WHITE-THROATED CAPUCHIN MONKE
Cebus capucinus

This monkey has a varied diet that consists mainly of fruits and insects but also includes small vertebrates and birds. It visits the forest floor only in search of water.

The Amazon forest, the largest tropical forest in the world, covers an area of approximately 3 million square miles (8 million sq km). Renowned for its tremendous biodiversity, it is home to about 2.5 million insects and some 2,000 species of birds and mammals. The rainforest is divided into four principal layers that span the considerable distance from the ground to the treetops, which can exceed 250 feet (about 75 meters). The four layers (forest floor, understory, canopy, and emergent layer) are sufficiently different from one another that they generate specific types of adaptations in plants as well as in animals. ●

The World in a Tree

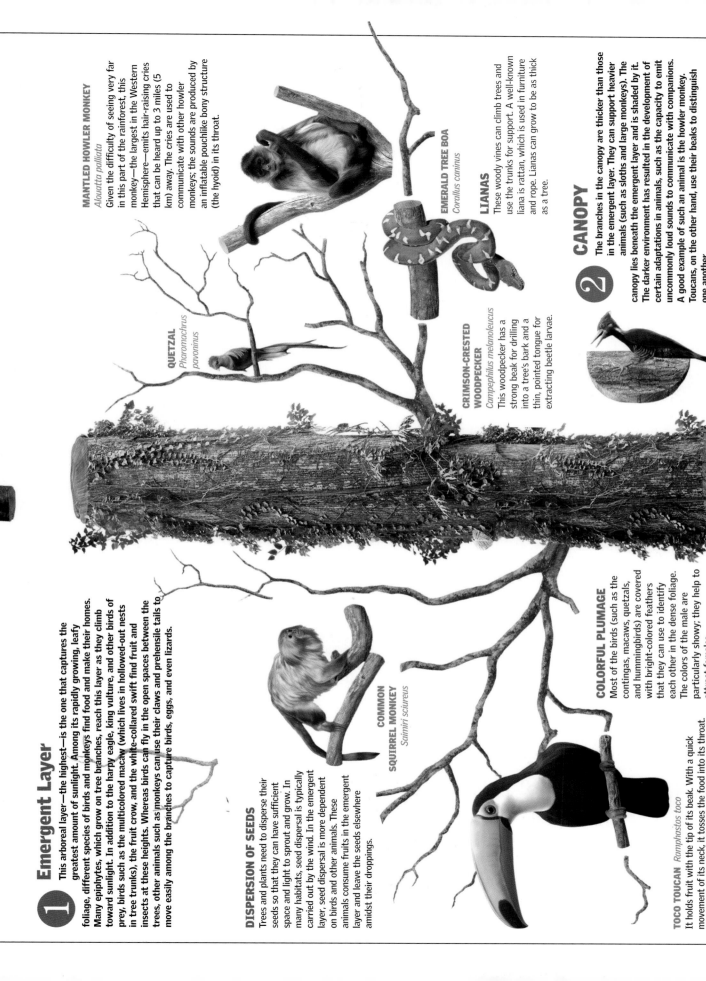

1 Emergent Layer

This arboreal layer—the highest—is the one that captures the greatest amount of sunlight. Among its rapidly growing, leafy foliage, different species of birds and monkeys find food and make their homes. Many epiphytes, which grow on tree branches, reach this layer as they climb toward sunlight. In addition to the harpy eagle, king vulture, and other birds of prey, birds such as the multicolored macaw (which lives in hollowed-out nests in tree trunks), the fruit crow, and the white-collared swift find fruit and insects at these heights. Whereas birds can fly in the open spaces between the trees, other animals such as monkeys can use their claws and prehensile tails to move easily among the branches to capture birds, eggs, and even lizards.

DISPERSION OF SEEDS

Trees and plants need to disperse their seeds so that they can have sufficient space and light to sprout and grow. In many habitats, seed dispersal is typically carried out by the wind. In the emergent layer, seed dispersal is more dependent on birds and other animals. These animals consume fruits in the emergent layer and leave the seeds elsewhere amidst their droppings.

TOCO TOUCAN *Ramphastos toco*
It holds fruit with the tip of its beak. With a quick movement of its neck, it tosses the food into its throat.

COMMON SQUIRREL MONKEY
Saimiri sciureus

COLORFUL PLUMAGE

Most of the birds (such as the contingas, macaws, quetzals, and hummingbirds) are covered with bright-colored feathers that they can use to identify each other in the dense foliage. The colors of the male are particularly showy; they help to attract females.

MANTLED HOWLER MONKEY
Alouatta palliata
Given the difficulty of seeing very far in this part of the rainforest, this monkey—the largest in the Western Hemisphere—emits hair-raising cries that can be heard up to 3 miles (5 km) away. The cries are used to communicate with other howler monkeys; the sounds are produced by an inflatable pouchlike bony structure (the hyoid) in its throat.

QUETZAL
Pharomachrus pavoninus

EMERALD TREE BOA
Corallus caninus

LIANAS

These woody vines can climb trees and use the trunks for support. A well-known liana is rattan, which is used in furniture and rope. Lianas can grow to be as thick as a tree.

2 CANOPY

The branches in the canopy are thicker than those in the emergent layer. They can support heavier animals (such as sloths and large monkeys). The canopy lies beneath the emergent layer and is shaded by it. The darker environment has resulted in the development of certain adaptations in animals, such as the capacity to emit uncommonly loud sounds to communicate with companions. A good example of such an animal is the howler monkey. Toucans, on the other hand, use their beaks to distinguish one another.

CRIMSON-CRESTED WOODPECKER
Campephilus melanoleucus
This woodpecker has a strong beak for drilling into a tree's bark and a thin, pointed tongue for extracting beetle larvae.

③ UNDERSTORY

In this shadowy zone, sunlight is limited. The layer is home to shrubs, thickets, and climbing plants, and many of these plants have red or dark green leaves. The understory functions as a transit zone for animals (such as bats, squirrels, monkeys, and snakes) that head either to the forest floor or to the emergent layer. Other animals in this layer include frogs. These amphibians use the small pools of water found in bromeliads to shelter their eggs and tadpoles.

SPECTACLED OWL
Pulsatrix perspicillata

Equipped with sharp claws, sharp eyesight, and exceptional hearing, this owl is adapted for low-light hunting. Its prey are mammals, tree frogs, and small insects. In contrast with other owls that patrol hunting territories while in flight, this species hunts from a tree limb and captures its prey on the ground or within the foliage.

SOUTH AMERICAN COATI
Nasua nasua

It hunts in groups that share food. It has strong limbs and claws similar to those of a bear, which it uses for climbing and digging. It can climb down from trees head first, thanks to its flexible joints. When it senses danger, it raises its long tail as a signal to other coatis.

PALM TREES

The lack of light in the understory lets only certain slow-developing palm trees grow.

EPIPHYTES

These plants begin life in the canopy, getting nutrients from the air, the rain, and the compost found on the tree branches that support them.

PALE-THROATED THREE-TOED SLOTH
Bradypus tridactylus

This animal spends virtually all its time in the trees. It only comes down from the trees to defecate. While fastened to the tree trunk, it digs a hole for its droppings and then covers them up. A type of algae grows on its fur that gives its brown coat a greenish cast, which serves as a camouflage. Moths, for their part, feed on the algae.

CLIMBING PLANTS

More than 2,500 species exist, and some can reach a length of 245 feet (75 meters). Some plants, such as the Rhaphidophora decursiva, have aerial roots that wind around the tree trunks to reach the light at the higher levels.

SOUTHERN TAMANDUA
Tamandua tetradactyla

It extracts its prey—ants and termites—by using its strong claws to break open their nests. A tamandua walks on the back part of its front paws in order to avoid poking its sharp nails into its palms. It captures its prey with the help of an elongated tongue that secretes a sticky liquid. The animal also likes honey and bees, which supplement the fruit and meat it eats.

POISON ARROW FROG
Dendrobates auratus

Because many of this frog's enemies, such as snakes and spiders, have developed a resistance to weak toxins, it defends itself by secreting chemicals based on very poisonous alkaloids through its skin. Its brilliant color warns predators of its toxicity. When the frog's eggs hatch, the male carries the tadpoles on its back and deposits them in small rain puddles, in tree cavities, or in epiphytes such as a bromeliad.

④ Forest Floor

The forest floor is relatively free of vegetation because the canopy casts deep shadows. The vigorous growth of plants on the forest floor only occurs when there is a break in the canopy. The canopy absorbs or reflects most of the sunlight, and only 5% penetrates to the forest floor.

Some mammals and birds, however, do not climb or fly. They include the small pudu deer, the armadillo, and the Ruddy dove. In addition, there are animals that are specifically found under the old leaves on the forest floor. These animals (such as cockroaches, beetles, centipedes, and earthworms), together with fungi and bacteria, feed on whatever falls from the levels above.

COLLARED PECCARY
Tayassu tajacu
This mammal lives in groups. It has a peculiar odor that is produced when its lumbar odoriferous gland is rubbed. The collared peccary resembles a wild boar, but it does not have exposed tusks.

JAGUAR
Panthera onca

Recycling The forest floor is surprisingly sparse in comparison with the richness of life that it supports. It is, however, a very dynamic place. Elevated temperatures and humidity promote the rapid decomposition of foliage that continually falls from the trees. This foliage is transformed by insects into a source of nutrition for the large trees. The roots of the trees engage in a symbiotic relationship with fungi.

TAYRA
Eira barbara
It has both tree- and ground-based behaviors, and it is a good climber and swimmer. It has a variable diet, eating everything from fruit to small animals (such as squirrels and birds). The tayra is hunted by jaguars. For safety, tayras commonly travel in pairs.

Temperate Forest

This type of forest occupies practically one-half of all forested lands on the planet. This biome ranges from cold, wintery regions to subtropical zones. The trees in this biome are usually deciduous (that is, they lose their foliage during the winter). Temperate forests have special adaptations to survive the winter. When spring arrives, the forest is enriched by a burst of varied and dynamic activity. In the warmest zones, the trees of the temperate forest keep their leaves the entire year round. ●

Perennial Forest

Also known as a sclerophyllic forest, this forest type is made up of trees with wide leaves. These leaves differ from those in a deciduous forest in that they grow in the winter when liquid water is available. These forests are found in California, western South America, the Mediterranean, and eastern and southeastern Australia. The open crowns typical of perennial trees allow the Sun's rays to shine through. Several ground-dwelling animals live in these forests. Perennial forests are very fragrant, owing to the oils that the trees produce.

SHORT-HORNED GRASSHOPPER
Acrididae
Varying in size between 0.4 and 3.2 inches (1–8 cm), some 10,000 species of grasshoppers have been identified throughout the world. Grasshoppers are herbivorous; they only eat plants. These insects can be detrimental to agriculture; they often gather in swarms to attack planted fields.

Life Strategies

In the spring and summer, life is relatively simple for most species. It is a period when food is more plentiful, and it is the most opportune time to breed and produce young. During the winter, unfortunately, the weather worsens, forcing many birds to migrate in search of better conditions; however, some birds and animals, such as rooks, woodpeckers, and red foxes, survive on stored food. The porcupine lives six months on the reserves of fat that its body accumulates. Some animals survive winter by hibernating.

PEREGRINE FALCON
Falco peregrinus
This falcon, a daytime flier, is one of the fastest birds in the world. These birds are capable of reaching a speed of 200 miles (320 km) per hour. The species is found on all the continents except Antarctica. Peregrine falcon populations decreased dramatically as a result of the use of DDT in the 1950s and 1960s.

KOALA
Phascolarctos cinereus
The koala spends most of its time climbing and sitting in eucalyptus trees, where it feeds at night during a four-hour period. It sometimes descends from the trees in order to help digest its food and supplement its diet with dirt, bark, and gravel. Despite its cuddly appearance, the koala will readily bite or scratch an intruder.

Deciduous Forest

The species of trees in this biome lose their leaves during the cold months of the year. In the autumn, the leaves fall to the ground in a thick layer. Insects, worms, and some small mammals use this layer of leaves as a place to hibernate. The winter season is often associated with desolate images devoid of animal life; however, the forest quickly regains its intensity in the spring. The deciduous forest then harbors a great variety of birds and other animal species.

Some of the most typical trees are the oak, beech, and elm. In humid areas, it is common to see these trees covered with green moss. The deciduous forest is the forest most characteristic of the Northern Hemisphere; it occurs on the east and west coasts of North America and in many regions throughout Europe and Asia.

NORTH AMERICAN GRAY SQUIRREL
Sciurus carolinensis

It is an opportunistic feeder, and its diet is made up of fruits, flowers, fungi, buds, nuts, and seeds, which it stores to eat during the winter. Its nest is typically built from branches, bark, and grass. Unlike the European squirrel, the North American gray squirrel has a gray back, and its underside is pale, white, or near-white. It was also introduced into Europe from North America.

RED, OR COMMON, FOX
Vulpes vulpes

This wide-ranging species is found in many temperate forests and can even be found in the Arctic. Active during the day and at night, the fox lives in caves and other hidden places, such as enlarged rabbit burrows or narrow spaces between rocks or beneath outbuildings on farms.

Arboreal Layers

The interlaced tree crowns form a layer called the canopy. In the summer, it is saturated with birds and insects. This canopy is typically deep but open, differing from that of other forests in the sense that sunlight can reach the understory and stimulate plant growth. In the summer, however, the abundance of leaves screens out most of the light, and only a little reaches the ground. On the forest floor, the fallen leaves—characteristic of oaks and other deciduous trees—form a soil covering that shelters one of the richest microhabitats in the world.

GREAT HORNED OWL
Bubo virginianus

The distinctive horns over its ears, along with its sharp beak, large wings, and powerful claws, give this enormous owl an intimidating appearance. Its keen vision and hearing make it an effective nighttime hunter, a job that it executes fiercely, quickly, and quietly. The bird is territorial and sedentary. Both the males and females look after their young, protecting their nest, which is usually built into the cavity of a tree.

EURASIAN BADGER
Meles meles

In contrast with other mustelids (that is, members of the weasel family), badgers live in clans of up to six members. They inhabit tunnels and underground chambers and defend a territory of up to 370 acres (150 hectares) in size. Although it has poor sight, the Eurasian badger has a keen sense of smell. Its striped face serves as camouflage.

Deciduous Forest

The species of trees, such as the oak, that grow in this type of forest produce foliage that falls during the cold months of the year. Great numbers of insects feed on abundant thin and easily consumed leaves during the spring and summer. Many birds also seek out deciduous trees for larva and worms that hide among the leaves, and some birds can even poke into the bark to feed on small animals that live within the trees. ●

BRAMBLING
Fringilla montifringilla
This bird, which makes a buzzing nasal sound, builds a cup-shaped nest lined with lichen, bark, roots, stems, hair, and feathers. Bramblings can gather into flocks of millions of birds.

RED FOX
Vulpes vulpes

EURASIAN BADGER
Meles meles

FALLOW DEER
Dama dama
It mainly eats grass and acorns. It travels in herds of 100 or more. Its dappled coat of fur provides camouflage from predators.

BURYING BEETLE
Nicrophorus investigator
It buries the bodies of small dead vertebrates whole. The burying beetle deposits its eggs in these buried carcasses.

SHEETWEB SPIDER
Lepthyphantes zelatus

MILLIPEDE
Ommatoiulus rutilans

EARTHWORM
Lombricus terrestris

WOOD LOUSE
Porcellio scaber

RECYCLING
Fungi are important organisms that hasten the decomposition of wood and the remains of plants and animals.

THE ROLE OF INVERTEBRATES
Insects, centipedes, nematodes, and other invertebrates that eat plants and decaying wood live beneath the fallen leaves in the forest. After a period of hibernation, the arrival of spring allows the insects to emerge in great numbers. They are the base of the forest's complex food web.

Fallen Leaves

Deciduous trees produce a deep layer of decomposing leaves rich in insects, fungi, and bacteria. These organisms provide vital nutrients to the soil by breaking down fallen leaves. As earthworms crawl through this matter, they ingest and later expel it. In doing so, they help mix buried and surface materials. Their tunnels also help aerate the soil and drain off rainwater. The transformation from fallen leaves to usable nutrients can last two years; it is a process that brings about the growth of new plants.

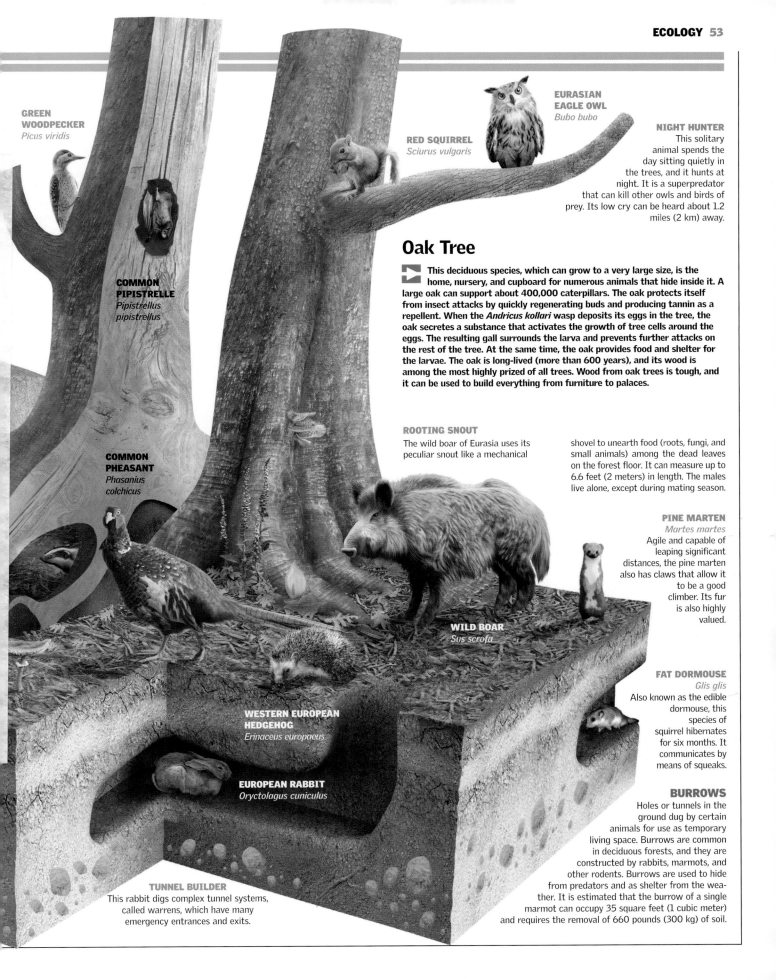

GREEN WOODPECKER
Picus viridis

COMMON PIPISTRELLE
Pipistrellus pipistrellus

COMMON PHEASANT
Phasanius colchicus

RED SQUIRREL
Sciurus vulgaris

EURASIAN EAGLE OWL
Bubo bubo

NIGHT HUNTER
This solitary animal spends the day sitting quietly in the trees, and it hunts at night. It is a superpredator that can kill other owls and birds of prey. Its low cry can be heard about 1.2 miles (2 km) away.

Oak Tree

This deciduous species, which can grow to a very large size, is the home, nursery, and cupboard for numerous animals that hide inside it. A large oak can support about 400,000 caterpillars. The oak protects itself from insect attacks by quickly regenerating buds and producing tannin as a repellent. When the *Andricus kollari* wasp deposits its eggs in the tree, the oak secretes a substance that activates the growth of tree cells around the eggs. The resulting gall surrounds the larva and prevents further attacks on the rest of the tree. At the same time, the oak provides food and shelter for the larvae. The oak is long-lived (more than 600 years), and its wood is among the most highly prized of all trees. Wood from oak trees is tough, and it can be used to build everything from furniture to palaces.

ROOTING SNOUT
The wild boar of Eurasia uses its peculiar snout like a mechanical shovel to unearth food (roots, fungi, and small animals) among the dead leaves on the forest floor. It can measure up to 6.6 feet (2 meters) in length. The males live alone, except during mating season.

PINE MARTEN
Martes martes
Agile and capable of leaping significant distances, the pine marten also has claws that allow it to be a good climber. Its fur is also highly valued.

WILD BOAR
Sus scrofa

WESTERN EUROPEAN HEDGEHOG
Erinaceus europaeus

EUROPEAN RABBIT
Oryctolagus cuniculus

FAT DORMOUSE
Glis glis
Also known as the edible dormouse, this species of squirrel hibernates for six months. It communicates by means of squeaks.

BURROWS
Holes or tunnels in the ground dug by certain animals for use as temporary living space. Burrows are common in deciduous forests, and they are constructed by rabbits, marmots, and other rodents. Burrows are used to hide from predators and as shelter from the weather. It is estimated that the burrow of a single marmot can occupy 35 square feet (1 cubic meter) and requires the removal of 660 pounds (300 kg) of soil.

TUNNEL BUILDER
This rabbit digs complex tunnel systems, called warrens, which have many emergency entrances and exits.

Coniferous Forest

Conifers are very hardy trees that are able to survive low temperatures and strong winds because of their tough, needlelike leaves. The needlelike shape of each leaf repels snow. A conifer's seeds, a valuable winter food source, form inside a cone that remains closed until it matures. Although most conifers are evergreens, some needles do fall off. When the needles fall, they make the soil acidic and reduce its quality. The trees protect themselves by growing close together, forming a dense stand. Coniferous forests are found from the cold northern latitudes and high mountain slopes to temperate and even tropical latitudes. ●

Temperate Rainforest

The most extensive areas of rainforest occur in the tropics, but rainforests also exist in temperate regions such as along the western coast of North America. The world's largest temperate rainforests are found in this region. The conifers in these forests can exceed 245 feet (75 meters) in height, and their trunks can be 10 feet (3 meters) or more in diameter. Unlike the boreal forest, this biome is relatively rare, and the climate is characterized by moderate temperatures. Moisture and temperature conditions in temperate rainforests are conducive for slugs and salamanders.

LEAST WEASEL
Mustela nivalis
It is active day and night, and it needs to eat the equivalent of one-third of its body weight each day in order to survive.

WARM-BLOODEDNESS
A property of certain groups of animals (such as birds and mammals) that allows them to maintain a constant body temperature independent of the temperature of the environment. Warm-bloodedness allows these animals to remain active in hot and cold temperatures.

930 miles (1,500 km)
the distance that some birds fly to find food in order to survive through harsh winters

COMMON BARN OWL
Tyto alba
This expert hunter has a distinctive heart-shaped face and dark eyes. Its vision and hearing are so highly developed that it can locate its prey at night. It feeds on rats and mice, which are swallowed whole.

NORTH AMERICAN PORCUPINE
Erethizon dorsatum
It is known for its array of long quills, up to 3.1 inches (8 cm) long. Even though it moves clumsily, it can climb trees in search of food. It is a noisy animal, especially during courtship; it whines, squeals, grunts, mews, and wails.

Arboreal Forest, or Taiga

This vast band of trees constitutes the widest expanse of forests in the world, covering around 5.8 million square miles (15 million sq km). It spans northern Russia and Siberia, northern Europe, Alaska, and the area around the Hudson Bay in northern Canada. The climate in this biome is very cold; however, its average summer temperature is 66° F (19° C). The fauna that inhabits this region is conditioned to live through long, hard winters. All animals here need to have good supplies of food to avoid freezing to death.

CANADIAN LYNX
Lynx canadensis
This lone hunter can successfully bring down prey as large as deer. It has thick pads of hair that grow beneath its feet; this allows it to move effortlessly over the snow.

BROWN BEAR
Ursus arctos
Known for its powerful frame and unpredictable behavior, the brown bear can be a threat to people and livestock. It tends to avoid human contact, but it will act aggressively to defend itself, especially when it has no place to seek refuge.

Hunting Packs

Gray wolves live in social groups called packs that occupy and defend large areas. Wolves mark their territory with their urine. Packs hunt large deer, moose, reindeer, or musk oxen—animals that can weigh 10 times more than an individual wolf. Within the hierarchy of the pack, the dominant breeding pair are the first to dine on captured prey. The wolves of the pack often display bonding behaviors, such as licking each other and wagging their tails.

WOLVERINE
Gulo gulo

The largest terrestrial mustelid, it is a stocky, solitary prowler that stalks its victims over the soft snow with the aid of its wide paws and strong legs. The wolverine's powerful jaws can grind frozen meat and bones. It also feeds on sick animals. It has a growl similar to the brown bear, which is ominous enough to scare away predators.

Taiga

The boreal forest, also called the taiga, is named after Boreas, Greek god of the north wind. Unlike other forests, it contains only a few species of coniferous trees, which are particularly adapted to withstand strong winds and low temperatures. The thick branches and needles of the trees cast heavy shadows, hampering the growth of other plants. The seeds of the trees are enclosed in cones that are covered by woody, protective scales. Although the seeds are difficult obtain, squirrels and other animals are able to extract them from the cones and store them for the winter. ●

BARN SWALLOW
Hirundo rustica

SCOTCH PINE
Pinus sylvestris
This pine tree is particularly hardy against frost, wind, and snow.

MOOSE
Alces alces
The largest animal of the deer family. Males use their antlers to fight other males during breeding season.

FELINE HUNTER
This carnivore can bring down hoofed animals four times its size

EURASIAN BADGER
Meles meles

EURASIAN LYNX
Lynx lynx

ACIDIC SOIL
Evergreen trees block much of the sunlight. Fallen pine needles increase the acidity of the soil. Consequently, tiny plants such as mosses and lichens dominate the forest floor.

EURASIAN BADGER
Meles meles
Badgers live in groups that reside in burrows made up of a large system of tunnels and chambers. Each tunnel complex may have as many as 10 entrances. Badgers cover their nests with a layer of dry grass, leaves, and moss. Despite poor vision, they have a keen sense of smell. The stripes on the badger's face can serve as camouflage or as marks that help group members identify each other.

RED KITE
Milvus milvus

AMUR LEOPARD
Panthera pardus orientalis

BROWN BEAR
Ursus arctos

RED FOX
Vulpes vulpes

MUSK DEER
Moschus moschiferus

MUSK GLAND
This small Siberian deer produces musk when it is in heat. It is a strong-smelling substance that attracts male musk deer. It is also used in making perfumes.

WOLVERINE
Gulo gulo

WILD BOAR
Sus scrofa

BURROWS
Inside its den, an animal can hibernate to survive the extreme cold of the taiga with a minimal expenditure of energy.

UNDERGROUND
A vole often shares tunnels made by other voles, and it digs chambers for shelter and food storage.

BANK VOLE
Clethrionomys glareolus

The Siberian Taiga

The taiga covers vast areas of Siberia. The long, severe winters of this region allow only a uniform stretch of coniferous trees to grow there. In northeastern Siberia, the temperature above the frozen ground can fall to almost –94° F (–70° C). The snowfall makes it difficult for trees to obtain water, but their needles inhibit moisture loss, and the needles remain green throughout the winter. Surprisingly, many animals (such as the wolverine, reindeer, bear, and red squirrel) live in this habitat, although the extreme conditions force some to migrate south or seek refuge underground. The arrival of spring reenergizes the pines, firs, and other trees, and the mosses and lichens reappear. The melting snow creates wet, spongy ground suitable for the development of insect eggs and ponds, where beavers, water rats, ducks, and cranes can find food.

Mountains

In contrast to habitats that have a more stable climate, temperatures in the mountains fall almost 9° F (5° C) for every 3,280 feet (1,000 meters) of elevation. In addition, the oxygen becomes thinner, the climate becomes drier, and the atmosphere filters out fewer ultraviolet rays. In spite of these conditions, the mountains are home to a large variety of organisms, many of which are largely distributed along its forested slopes. In the higher regions, where low-growing plants, boulders, and snow-covered peaks can be found, there may be fewer predators, because special adaptations to the conditions are required. ●

Tropical Mountains

The warm climate of tropical regions spurs the growth of vegetation, even at high elevations, and trees can be found at 13,000 feet (4,000 meters). At even higher elevations, there are animals such as the vicuña and Andean hummingbird. The small size of the Andean hummingbird hinders its ability to hold enough energy to survive the night. During the winter nights, this bird often falls into torpor, a state of lowered body temperature and metabolism. Tropical mountain forests are often covered in clouds. Cloud forests shelter a number of animals facing extinction, including the mountain gorilla and the quetzal.

ANDEAN BEAR
Tremarctos ornatus

It is also known as a spectacled bear because of the white coloration around its eyes. It is a vegetarian with large jaws and molars, and thus it can eat even the toughest of plants. The Andean bear also makes strange vocalizations.

VICUÑA
Vicugna vicugna

This grazing animal uses its split, prehensile upper lip to pull the grasses that it eats out of the ground. Its blood has a high oxygen capacity, and it can climb to high elevations to graze. It is territorial and uses its droppings as a marker. The vicuña is native to the Andes of South America.

The Oxygen Problem

Many animals that live in the mountains have developed the ability to improve the oxygen capacity of their blood. Birds have a unidirectional respiratory system that some birds of the Himalayas use to fly at 26,000 feet (8,000 meters). Mammals such as the vicuña, on the other hand, become acclimatized through an increase in red blood cells, which improves oxygen transport.

MOUNTAIN GORILLA
Gorilla beringei beringei

Its fur, unlike that of other gorillas, is long and unkempt, which helps it retain body heat at 13,000 feet (4,000 meters). It lives in groups of up to 40 members, which include one silverback (male) gorilla and several females and offspring.

The silverback will yawn when it is nervous and will bark and stare in defense. The mountain gorilla is basically herbivorous, but it can also eat larvae, ants, and snails. It is in constant danger from poachers.

Temperate Mountains

Even though the climate is more stable, the arrival of spring produces significant growth in the plants of the high mountains. Spring also prompts many animals in search of food to climb upward to areas normally inhabited by birds of prey. The vulture known as the bonebreaker carries the bones of dead animals to great heights before dropping them. When the bones strike the ground, they break open, and the bonebreaker vulture can then eat the marrow. Other animals, such as the marmot, simply leave their burrows to enjoy the fruits of the season. In mountain forests of lower elevations, where conditions are warmer, there are mountain lions, bears, deer, and a large variety of birds.

YAK
Bos grunniens

This large bovid, which is native to the Himalayas, lives at elevations as high as 20,000 feet (6,000 meters). It chews ice as a source of water. It has no predators, although bears have been known to attack it on rare occasions. Yaks have been domesticated and are used as beasts of burden. They are valued as a source of milk, wool, and meat.

YELLOW-BELLIED MARMOT
Marmota flaviventris

This rodent easily adjusts to its habitat. It primarily eats seeds, grasses, flowers, and herbs, and it lives in groups that are generally made up of a single male and several females. The yellow-bellied marmot can hibernate for up to eight months in burrows, which are excavated by male marmots. It is active during the day, and it spends most of its time searching for food.

Migrations

In the temperate mountains, unlike the mountains in the tropics, winter is a critical time that reduces the supply of food. Some animals, such as insects, need to hibernate, entering a deep lethargy that slows their metabolic activity. Many animals move to lower, and thus warmer, elevations. The mating seasons of mountain goats and reindeer coincide with this vertical migration, and some animal species migrate past the wooded mountain slopes down to sea level.

IBEX
Capra ibex

It lives in elevations up to 22,000 feet (6,700 meters). It has thick, curved horns that have the shape of a scimitar. Male ibexes use their horns to compete for control of a flock and its females. The males gather together and, like wild goats, lift themselves on their hind legs while they crash their enormous horns against each other to determine the dominant male. Their fur thickens and changes color in preparation for winter.

SNOW LEOPARD
Panthera uncial

This feline with shaggy fur can live in habitats as high as 16,500 feet (5,000 meters) above sea level. Except during mating season, it is a solitary animal. The fur of the snow leopard serves as camouflage among the rocky slopes while it lies in wait for prey. In addition, it has powerful jaws and short, robust limbs suitable for climbing trees. Prey not immediately devoured are placed in trees. It hunts during the day and will attack prey both smaller and larger than itself. Several prey species (such as hares, marmots, goats, and even yaks) make up its diet.

Temperate Mountains

The Himalayan mountain system contains the highest mountains in the world. The highest, Mount Everest, has an elevation of 29,035 feet (8,850 meters). Blizzards, fog, and hurricane winds are examples of the adverse weather conditions that occur there. Yaks and a few other animals can live above 20,000 feet (6,000 meters). Nevertheless, differences in temperature, air quality, and oxygen levels, which vary with elevation, affect the development of many species, even those far from the perpetual snow. ●

COMMON KESTREL
Falco tinnunculus

COMMON KINGFISHER
Alcedo atthis Its beak is quite pointed, which makes it particularly useful for catching fish. After diving into the water, its streamlined wings allow it to burst out of the water quickly.

EURASIAN BROWN BEAR *Ursus arctos*
It uses its large claws to dig up roots and bulbs. In the winter, this bear typically takes refuge in an underground mountain den, where it can remain for up to six months. Because it cannot lower its body temperature, it lives off its reserves of fat during the winter.

ADAPTATIONS

The Himalayas, like the Arctic, are a very hostile environment for animals; however, 28 species of mammals—from the hairy yak to the diminutive pica—manage to cope with the hard winters. These mammals survive with the help of their fur or their ability to find and make shelters. In springtime, the high-country meadows draw many herbivorous goatlike animals, including the Siberian ibex and the Himalayan tahr.

NATIVE SPECIES

The snow leopard, the Himalayan mole, and the Himalayan tahr are unique to the Himalayas.

STRATIFIED LANDSCAPE

The mountainous terrain is far from uniform. Below the 15,000-foot (4,500-meter) snow-capped peaks and rocky slopes of bare black granite, there are places where mosses, lichens, herbs, and low shrubs (such as the *Saussurea* and *Rhododendron*) grow. The arrival of spring melts the snows and triggers the appearance of alpine flowers (such as gentian, saxifrage, and primrose). From 11,500 feet (3,500 meters) downward, there are forests of blue pine, cedar, birch, and juniper.

HIMALAYAN PIKA
Ochotona himalayana

COMMON BARBERRY
Berberis vulgaris

Insects

At high altitudes, plants attract thousands of insects. Such insects include bristletails, flies, butterflies, and many species of beetles (such as the ladybug and stag beetle). At the same time, many birds feed on the insects. Other invertebrates (such as centipedes, spiders, and earwigs) hide beneath rocks as they seek spores from lichens and mosses.

CLICK BEETLE

STAG BEETLE
Lucanus cervus

SEVEN-SPOTTED LADYBIRD
Coccinella septempunctata

RHESUS MONKEY *Macaca mulatta* This monkey is sacred to Hindus. It was the first primate to be launched into space, and it has been commonly used as a laboratory animal.

PEREGRINE FALCON
Falco peregrinus

HIMALAYAN VULTURE
Gyps himalayensis

BEAR HUNTING
The black bear can spend half its time in trees. It is sought after by hunters, especially for its gall bladder, which is used in Asian cuisines and various medications.

DROMEDARY
Camelus dromedarius

ASIATIC BLACK BEAR
Ursus thibetanus

HIMALAYAN SEROW
Capricornis thar

AGILITY Despite its slowness, the serow is able to climb rocky slopes to escape predators and to seek shelter during the cold winters and hot summers.

YAK
Bos grunniens

SUBSISTENCE The milk and meat of the yak has sustained Tibetans for millennia. In addition to being a source of food, the yak is important in Tibetan Buddhist rituals, which include offerings of yak butter. Yak meat is as tender as beef but is richer in nutrients.

Polar Regions

The Arctic and the Antarctic—the regions bounded by the polar circles—are the coldest habitats on Earth. Each region is characterized by periods of 24-hour sunlight in the summer and 24-hour darkness in the winter. The Arctic is a largely ice-covered ocean that is enclosed by extensive areas of tundra. The tundra is used by some animals for grazing. Antarctica, on the other hand, is a continent that lies completely beneath a vast covering of ice; it is surrounded by the stormiest seas in the world. ●

KRILL
Euphausia superba
This crustacean of the open ocean, only 2.4 inches (6 cm) long, is an essential link in the food chain. Krill are food sources for many whales, penguins, and fish.

Antarctica

Isolated from the rest of the world, Antarctica is covered by a thick layer of ice up to 13,000 feet (4,000 meters) thick. The sparse vegetation does not support land animals. The Southern Ocean, which surrounds the continent, however, is one of the richest and most productive in the world. Here, individual swarms of krill can weigh as much as 10 million tons. Algae and lichens grow along Antarctica's coast during the summer, but larger plants can survive only on the Antarctic Peninsula.

EMPEROR PENGUIN
Aptenodytes forsteri

The emperor penguin is the world's largest penguin. It can endure very low winter temperatures, and it is capable of diving to a depth of about 1,750 feet (530 meters). The reproductive behavior of emperor penguins is unusual; in the winter, after laying one egg, the female heads for the sea and does not return until spring, when the chick is born. During the female's absence, the male holds the egg on his feet within a pocket of feathered skin that protects the egg from the cold.

2,900 square miles (7,600 sq km)

is the size of Antarctica's ice-free area. Antarctica is the world's fourth-largest continent.

Life under the Ice

Whales and seals need to dive to find food and must rise to the surface to breathe. In the winter, however, ice that forms on the surface of the ocean limits access to the air. It is for this reason that many species migrate to lower latitudes. The animals that do not leave the polar regions, such as seals, need to maintain breathing holes in sea ice. Frozen breathing holes can be as much as 6.5 feet (2 meters) thick.

LEOPARD SEAL
Hydrurga leptonyx
Unlike other seals, this solitary predator (also known as a sea leopard) swims by using its front flippers. It uses its wide jaws and strong teeth to sieve food from the water. It is a carnivorous mammal that, in addition to feeding on krill and squid, is proficient at hunting penguins.

HUMPBACK WHALE
Megaptera novaeangliae

This whale lives near coastal areas. In the spring, it migrates from the tropics to the Arctic Ocean and the Southern Ocean surrounding Antarctica. Even though it does not have vocal chords, it can produce a song—sometimes considered the most complex and richest of any animal in the world—to attract females or warn other males. The song may also serve as a kind of radar to detect other whales.

ICE CAP
The ice cap that covers Antarctica is 50% larger than the United States. Some studies show that the ice on part of this continent is melting, whereas others indicate that Antarctica is the one major body of ice on the Earth that is gaining ice mass rather than losing it.

The Arctic and Tundra

The Arctic Ocean, the world's smallest and shallowest ocean, is covered for most of the year by a thick layer of floating ice. Despite the difficult conditions, the coasts adjacent to this ocean are inhabited by people such as the Inuit. The Arctic is surrounded by a monotonous expanse of flat, treeless land called the tundra. The ground beneath the surface is permanently frozen. This underground layer of ice, or permafrost, prevents meltwater from draining off. As a result, pools of water are available in a region characterized by little snow or rain. In the summer, the top layer of underground ice melts, and the rapidly growing grasses and flowers attract herds of reindeer and other animals in search of food.

POLAR BEAR *Ursus maritimus*

This icon of the Arctic is the largest member of the carnivores. It has a streamlined body characterized by exceptional strength and stamina. The males can weigh twice as much as the females. Its long fur can even keep its paws warm while it walks on ice. In addition, a thick layer of fat protects it from the cold while swimming. Polar bears can hear prey below ice more than 3.3 feet (1 meter) thick and can smell beached whale carcasses up to 3 miles (5 km) away. Their principal prey are seals. Female polar bears feed their young in dens that are dug from the snow. A reduction in Arctic ice could drastically curtail their access to food.

Summer Migration

The summer daylight in the tundra lasts 24 hours a day, creating favorable conditions for the growth of plants. The plants draw animals such as geese (which pull up plants with their bills), wading birds (which feed on worms and insects), and other birds that find food in the water near shore. A similar phenomenon occurs in the ocean. Many blue whales arrive to take advantage of the resurgence of plankton.

MUSK OX *Ovibos moschatus*

The name of this animal comes from the strong odor that the male gives off during mating season. It has a double coat: an external coat of hair from which rain and snow slide off and an internal coat of fine hair that provides good insulation. Musk ox populations are low in some places, but they are recovering through reintroduction programs.

CAMOUFLAGE

The absence of any trees on the tundra makes camouflage a valuable adaptation. Often, it is the only means available to animals seeking protection in the landscape or is an advantage when they attack their prey. The changes in the landscape between summer and winter are so different that the Arctic fox changes its color. Its fur is a grayish brown in the summer, and it turns white in the fall.

1,000 miles (1,600 km)
the approximate distance that separates the magnetic North Pole from the geographic North Pole

ARCTIC FOX *Alopex lagopus*

The white, heavy fur of this small fox is good camouflage against the snow and ice in winter. During the summer, its coat thins by half and turns to gray or grayish brown. The Arctic fox makes its lair in an extensive system of burrows. The burrow provides shelter and a place for it to raise its young. The timing of the birth of its litter is closely linked to the amount of available food.

Between the Tundra and the Arctic

The Arctic is the region that extends from the North Pole to a band of trees called the taiga. The Arctic Ocean is covered with ice during the winter, creating conditions that many animals find too difficult to contend with. These animals migrate southward to a region called the tundra, where there is vegetation on which they can feed. In the summer, however, the ice along the shoreline begins to melt, spurring the rapid growth of plankton populations in the ocean. The sudden increase in this food source draws many marine animals, such as belugas, narwhals, killer whales, seals, shrimp, herring, cod, and plaice. ●

The Tundra

In the winter, the land that encircles the Arctic Ocean is largely lifeless; very few animals and plants overwinter here. Once the snow melts with the arrival of summer, however, the tundra flourishes with plants (such as mosses, lichens, algae, and many bushes). Many flowering plants also thrive. Animals follow. They include reindeer, polar bears, wolverines, and bald eagles. The muddy ponds formed from the melting ice bring out insects such as mosquitoes, which serve as a source of food for migratory birds. Beneath the ground and covered with lichens and mosses lies the hidden layer of ice called permafrost. It remains solid all year round.

SUMMER GRAZING
The tundra soil grows grasses that are suitable for the musk ox. This animal is so named because of its particular odor.

MUSK OX
Ovibos moschatus

REINDEER
Rangifer tarandus
In the spring, groups of wild reindeer migrate toward the tundra where they feed on grass and lichens and reproduce. Some travel 750 miles (1,200 km) two times each year.

BALD EAGLE
Haliaeetus leucocephalus

SNOWY OWL
Nyctea scandiaca
Its white plumage covers its body and even its beak to insulate the bird from the cold. The mottled pattern is characteristic of female snowy owls and blends in with the rocky ground where they lay their eggs.

ARCTIC FOX
Alopex lagopus

BIGHORN SHEEP
Ovis dalli

ARCTIC HARE
Lepus arcticus

POLAR BEAR
Ursus maritimus

WALRUS
Odobenus rosmarus

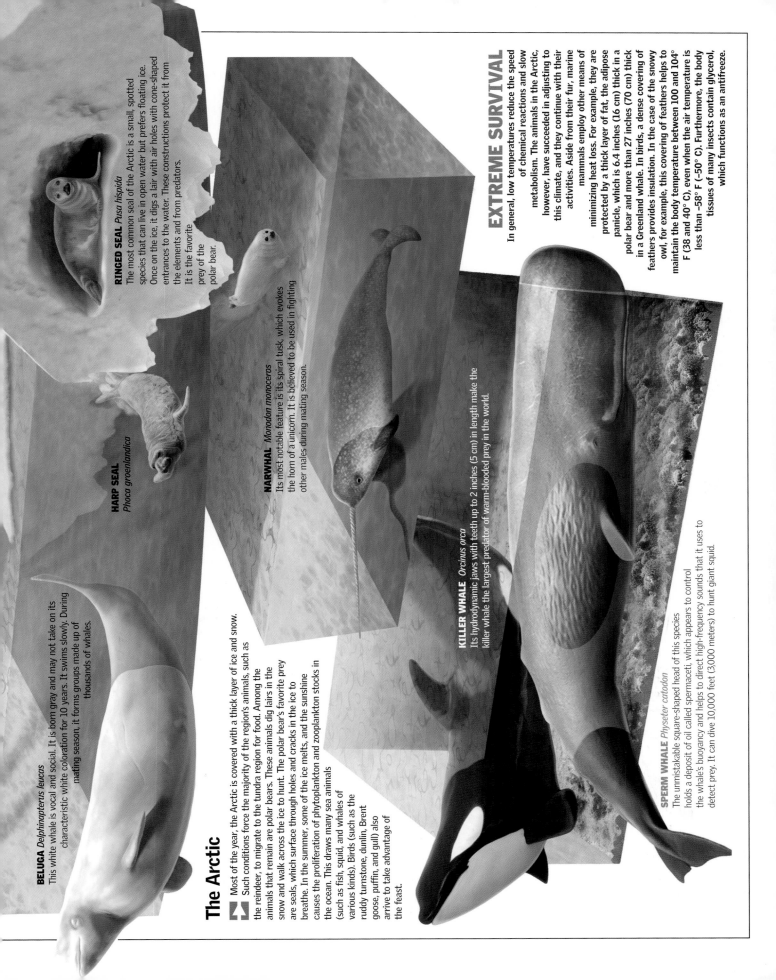

BELUGA *Delphinapterus leucas*
This white whale is vocal and social. It is born gray and may not take on its characteristic white coloration for 10 years. It swims slowly. During mating season, it forms groups made up of thousands of whales.

HARP SEAL *Phoca groenlandica*

RINGED SEAL *Pusa hispida*
The most common seal of the Arctic is a small, spotted species that can live in open water but prefers floating ice. Once on the ice, it digs a lair with air holes with cone-shaped entrances to the water. These constructions protect it from the elements and from predators. It is the favorite prey of the polar bear.

The Arctic

Most of the year, the Arctic is covered with a thick layer of ice and snow. Such conditions force the majority of the region's animals, such as the reindeer, to migrate to the tundra region for food. Among the animals that remain are polar bears. These animals dig lairs in the snow and walk across the ice to hunt. The polar bear's favorite prey are seals, which surface through holes and cracks in the ice to breathe. In the summer, some of the ice melts, and the sunshine causes the proliferation of phytoplankton and zooplankton stocks in the ocean. This draws many sea animals (such as fish, squid, and whales of various kinds). Birds (such as the ruddy turnstone, dunlin, Brent goose, puffin, and gull) also arrive to take advantage of the feast.

NARWHAL *Monodon monoceros*
Its most notable feature is its spiral tusk, which evokes the horn of a unicorn. It is believed to be used in fighting other males during mating season.

KILLER WHALE *Orcinus orca*
Its hydrodynamic jaws with teeth up to 2 inches (5 cm) in length make the killer whale the largest predator of warm-blooded prey in the world.

SPERM WHALE *Physeter catodon*
The unmistakable square-shaped head of this species holds a deposit of oil called spermaceti, which appears to control the whale's buoyancy and helps to direct high-frequency sounds that it uses to detect prey. It can dive 10,000 feet (3,000 meters) to hunt giant squid.

EXTREME SURVIVAL

In general, low temperatures reduce the speed of chemical reactions and slow metabolism. The animals in the Arctic, however, have succeeded in adjusting to this climate, and they continue with their activities. Aside from their fur, marine mammals employ other means of minimizing heat loss. For example, they are protected by a thick layer of fat, the adipose panicle, which is 6.4 inches (16 cm) thick in a polar bear and more than 27 inches (70 cm) thick in a Greenland whale. In birds, a dense covering of feathers provides insulation. In the case of the snowy owl, for example, this covering of feathers helps to maintain the body temperature between 100 and 104° F (38 and 40° C), even when the air temperature is less than –58° F (–50° C). Furthermore, the body tissues of many insects contain glycerol, which functions as an antifreeze.

Life in the Water

From above, water is just water. Once we enter the water, however, it is possible to discover a diversity of environments and ecosystems as rich as those we see on land. We will explore the coral reef, which like the rainforests on land, is a site of significant biodiversity. We will immerse ourselves in the waters of the open sea and visit the mysterious

SHOWY CORALS
Because of their enormous biodiversity,
coral reefs are the aquatic equivalents
of rainforests on land. Rising ocean
temperatures, however, are affecting
their overall health.

depths of the ocean trenches that
abound with strange creatures and
veritable sea monsters. We will learn
about one of the world's richest and
most complex environments—the
estuary. Here fresh water from a river
meets the salt water of the ocean to
create an explosion of life. Later, rivers,
lakes, and lagoons will reveal their
unique underwater world. ●

Aquatic Ecosystems

Water is vital for life. These ecosystems, marine and freshwater, cover a large percentage of the Earth's surface. The oceans contain more than 325 million cubic miles (1,350 million cu km) of water and enough salt to bury Europe to a depth of 3 miles (5 km). The oceans function as enormous boilers that distribute heat from the Sun over the entire planet. The freshwater ecosystems, for their part, supply water for drinking, household use, and irrigation. ●

Fresh water

Freshwater ecosystems have low concentrations of salt—generally less than 1%. They support 700 species of fish, 1,200 species of amphibians, and a variety of mollusks and insects. Their flora and fauna vary in relation to such factors as the chemical composition of the water, the presence of oxygen, strong water currents, and the timing of periodic droughts. Freshwater ecosystems can be divided into two principal types: standing-water ecosystems (such as lakes, ponds, and wetlands) and flowing-water ecosystems (such as streams and rivers).

SUBMERGED SURFACE

The average depth of the oceans is 12,450 feet (3,795 meters), and their deepest point is the Challenger Deep, in the Marianas Trench, 35,814 feet (10,916 meters) below sea level. That depth exceeds the height of the tallest mountain on the Earth's surface, Mount Everest, which has a height of 29,035 feet (8,850 meters) above sea level.

GREATEST DEPTH:
Marianas Trench
(Challenger Deep)
35,814 feet (10,916 meters)

AVERAGE ELEVATION OF EARTH'S ENTIRE SURFACE:
7,900 feet (2,400 meters)

HIGHEST POINT:
Mount Everest
29,035 feet
(8,850 meters)

Sea coasts

The meeting of land and sea produces a unique biodiversity, supported by the variety of food present, which is much greater than that of the open ocean. The physical features of the coast are constantly changing because of erosion from ocean waves, coastal currents that carry sand and gravel, and the ebb and flow of the tides. When the tide is low, organisms make adjustments to avoid dehydration. Anemones, for example, draw in their tentacles to become nothing but gelatinous protuberances. Some coastal areas have coral reefs, which are notable for their extraordinary forms and colors. Although beaches of sand, mud, or gravel have fewer ecological resources than do rocky coasts, the former are often used by animals as sites of nest building and shelter from predators.

WATER CYCLE

Water enters an area as precipitation and returns to the atmosphere through evaporation. Some of the water infiltrates the ground. What is left over flows toward bodies of water.

2 PRECIPITATION
As the air continues to condense, it forms droplets of water and flakes of snow.

1 EVAPORATION AND CONDENSATION
Rising air cools, and the water vapor condenses to form clouds.

3 CIRCULATION AND RETURN TO THE SEA
The falling water forms lakes and rivers that discharge into the ocean.

CONSTANT MOTION

Some 270 million years ago, Earth's land surface was joined together into a single continent, Pangaea, which was surrounded by water. It later broke into several tectonic plates. As these plates slowly shifted, they progressively reshaped the continents and oceans. Many of the borders between the plates, which continue in constant motion, extend along the ocean bottom. On the borders between two plates, the plates may move away from each other (as in mid-ocean rift zones, where new oceanic crust is formed from rising magma), may move toward each other (as in oceanic trenches, where one plate sinks beneath another), or may slide alongside each other.

The Nature of Sea Salt

The salts in the ocean are composed of a mixture of ions (that is, charged particles) of sodium, chlorine, sulfur, magnesium, potassium, and calcium. Some ions have a positive charge, and others have a negative charge.

Some of the salt ions come from rivers, which carry dissolved salts from rocks to the ocean, whereas others come from hydrothermal vents in the ocean floor. A third source of salt ions is from wind-carried volcanic ash. There are different natural processes by which a portion of each type of ion is removed from the ocean, but the most common ions remain dissolved in the ocean. These ions may remain in the ocean from a few centuries up to millions of years.

EASY FLOTATION

In closed seas, such as the Dead Sea, the water is so salty and dense that it makes submersion in the water difficult..

SALT WATER

The average salinity of the ocean is about 35 parts per thousand, although this value varies considerably at the ocean surface. Sources of water, such as rainfall and rivers, reduce the salinity of the ocean, while processes that remove water, such as evaporation, increase it. The freezing point of ocean water depends on its salinity. As salinity increases, the freezing point of water decreases. The salty taste of ocean water is the result of the large amount of chloride it contains.

TYPES OF SALT

The water of the marine ecosystems contains other salts in addition to sodium chloride, such as sulfates and chlorides of magnesium, calcium, and potassium in fixed proportions.

2.5% Other salts
4.4% Gypsum
15.8% Manganese salts
77.3% Sodium chloride (halite)

UNDERWATER PRESSURE

The pressure of the water increases about one bar for every 33 feet (10 meters) of depth. This fact creates a challenge for undersea scientific explorers, who must undergo slow decompression when they ascend.

Sea level
1 Atmosphere

33 feet (10 meters)
2 Atmospheres

66 feet (20 meters)
3 Atmospheres

Open Ocean

Some organisms live on or just under the surface of the ocean, which has optimal conditions of light and temperature. These organisms are called the neuston. Below the surface, the ocean is divided into four zones—the photic, aphotic, abyssal, and hadal. Each zone corresponds to levels of light and temperature, and these determine the specific kinds of adaptations we see in animals. The most difficult conditions are in the aphotic and abyssal zones because food becomes scarce. In addtion, animals in these zones need to retain liquid within their bodies to keep them from being compressed. At depths below about 20,000 feet (6,000 meters), there are ocean trenches that contain hydrothermal vents and strange fish that can withstand the high pressure of the surrounding water.

WATER	OTHER
Gas	Gas
Ice	Liquid
Liquid	Solid

DENSITY

Contrary to what might be expected, liquid water is more dense than ice (solid water). Water vapor (a gas) is less dense.

Oceans

From the time of their formation some four billion years ago, the oceans have constituted the largest continuous habitat in the world. The uneven relief of the ocean floor includes vast plains, mountain ranges, erupting volcanoes, and trenches that reach depths of more than 6 miles (10 km). The ocean is not uniform; pressure, dissolved oxygen content, light quality, and brightness all vary by location and time of year. Sea life is found at the surface and also in the deepest waters, where researchers continue to explore. ●

Ocean Currents

The movement of water in the ocean is driven by winds and density variations of the water, producing waves, tides, and large currents. In addition, water is diverted by sea coasts, seafloor topography, and Earth's rotation. Ocean currents affect the climate, physical relief, and wildlife of the coasts. They carry warm water from equatorial regions to the poles. Without these currents, the Earth's poles would become colder and the tropics would become warmer. The two basic types of currents are surface currents and deep-ocean currents. Ocean currents can also be classified according to temperature or other physical characteristics (as in tidal, wave, turbidity, or density currents).

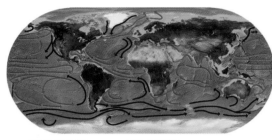

WARM CURRENTS → COLD CURRENTS →

SURFACE CURRENTS
Generated by the wind, these currents affect only 10% of the water in the ocean. They have an important effect on climate: they transfer heat from the tropics to colder regions. Surface currents can be more than 50 miles (80 km) wide with temperatures ranging from 28 to 86° F (–2 to 30° C). They follow a generally circular path. Surface currents flow clockwise in the Northern Hemisphere and counterclockwise in the Southern Hemisphere.

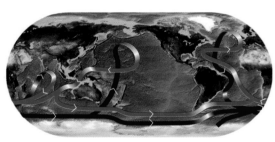

WARM CURRENTS → COLD CURRENTS →

DEEP-OCEAN CURRENTS
Deep-ocean currents are driven by thermohaline circulation. This type of circulation is driven by changes in water temperature and salinity (saltiness). Colder, saltier water is more dense. As it sinks, it is replaced by less dense, warmer water. Thermohaline circulation circles the globe and is an important factor in maintaining Earth's climate.

Hydrothermal Chimneys

This structure, which can be 200 feet (60 meters) high, emits a jet of extremely hot water from fissures in volcanic regions of the ocean floor. The pressure at these depths prevents the water from boiling; however, the jet of water can rise with great force. Deposits of sulfur and other minerals form around the chimney. The process sustains a rich and unusual biological community that includes bacteria, tube worms, squat lobsters, viviparous blennies, eyeless crabs, clams, mussels, and strange creatures called siphonophores, which are related to jellyfish.

CHEMOSYNTHESIS
The giant tube worms are supported by colonies of bacteria that live inside their bodies. The bacteria make food for the tube worms from chemical reactions involving hydrogen sulfide.

CONTINENTAL SHELF
It extends under water from the continental shore.

DISCOVERY
The first underwater or "black smoker" chimneys were discovered in the Galápagos Islands in 1977. Later, others were found along the midocean ridges of the eastern Pacific, central Atlantic, and northeast Pacific Oceans.

UNDERWATER EXPLORATION
Following the deep dives made by the crewed submersibles *Alvin* (14,800 feet [4,500 meters]) and *Shinkai* (21,300 feet [6,500 meters]), future Deep Flight submersibles will have inverted wings for rapid descent.

Relief of the Ocean Floor

Some mountains are found on land, but others occur at the bottom of the oceans. In addition, beyond the continental shelves and between depths from 13,000 to 19,500 feet (4,000 to 6,000 meters), there are large, flat regions, called abyssal plains, that are covered by sediments. Mid-ocean ridges cut through these plains. These ridges are found along the borders between tectonic plates. The ridges are essentially huge mountain chains formed by magma that rises from the space between the plates. In other areas of the ocean floor, where one tectonic plate slides beneath another, trenches more than 6 miles (10 km) deep occur.

Light and Sound

Although the water in the ocean is somewhat transparent, on a sunny day it appears to be blue. As light travels through the water, blue and green wavelengths are reflected, whereas the other wavelengths in the visible range are absorbed. Sound travels faster and farther under water than in the air. This quality is helpful to cetaceans such as dolphins and whales, because they rely on their vocalizations to communicate with one another.

ABSORPTION
The red and orange wavelengths of sunlight are absorbed within the first 50 feet (15 meters) of the ocean. Most of the rest is absorbed in the following 130 feet (40 meters).

SEAMOUNTS
Are underwater mountains that rise more than 3,300 feet (1,000 meters) from their bases. Those that have flat tops are called guyots.

ABYSSAL PLAIN
It lies between the continental shelf and the undersea mountains.

MID-OCEAN RIDGE
It forms where two tectonic plates separate.

Ocean Trenches

These deep, narrow valleys have a "V" shape. Trenches are the result of subduction, the process by which one plate of the Earth's crust slides beneath another when they collide. This process works in tandem with the expansion of the sea floor at the mid-ocean ridges. The trenches are between 6,500 and 13,000 feet (2,000 and 4,000 meters) deeper than the surrounding sea floor and form the hadal zone of the ocean. Despite very high pressures and cold temperatures in this region, exotic organisms thrive. This community includes sea cucumbers, anemones, crustaceans, and some mollusks. Most trenches are found along the borders of plates on the floor of the Pacific Ocean. A few smaller ocean trenches exist in the Indian and Atlantic Oceans.

OCEAN TRENCH
In 1960, the submersible *Trieste*, crewed by the scientists Jacques Piccard and Donald Walsh, descended to 35,810 feet (10,916 meters) in the Marianas Trench in the Pacific Ocean. The Trieste holds the record for the deepest descent.

Life in the Oceans

The first marine species emerged more than one billion years ago. Since then, life in the oceans has become progressively more complex. Today, it is a very diverse environment. The ocean can be divided into horizontal regions that correspond to polar, temperate, and tropical ecosystems and into vertically separated zones, or layers, that correspond to different depths. The deepest layer, the hadal zone, is the least understood. Some parts of the ocean have their own particular, or endemic, species. ●

Geographic Zones

→ Marine communities are distributed unevenly. They follow horizontal patterns that are arranged into polar, temperate, and tropical ecosystems. Climate and food availability are the principal factors that determine where the communities are located and the biodiversity they possess. Even though there is life at all depths, most of it is found in those zones in which the pressure, temperature, and illumination are favorable. A boundary between masses of water with different temperature and salinity characteristics forms a barrier that is as effective as mountains on the Earth's surface. Below a certain depth, however, these barriers diminish, and conditions are more stable and uniform. Consequently, organisms living in the abyssal zone have very wide distributions.

ENDEMIC SPECIES

These species are unique to particular geographic areas. They are found nowhere else. For example, the porcupine fish *Diodon hystrix* is endemic to the tropical waters of the western Atlantic Ocean.

CHANGES IN TEMPERATURE

Global warming is a phenomenon affecting the distribution of many species. For example, warm-water fish have now been found in cold ocean zones.

■ EQUATORIAL   ■ SUBTROPICAL   ■ POLAR AND SUBPOLAR

■ TROPICAL   ■ TEMPERATE

UNDERWATER EXPLORATION

→ Present-day technology allows crewed and remote-controlled submersibles to carry out detailed research at great depths. In 2006, the China Ocean Mineral Resources R&D Association (COMRA) began to test a crewed vehicle that can dive to 23,000 feet (7,000 meters). As technology imprves, next-generation submersibles will no longer depend on ballast and flotation tanks. *Deep Flight II*, designed by the American engineer Graham Hawkes, will use inverted wings to generate "negative lift" for rapid descent.

OCEANIC ZONES

1

PHOTIC ZONE

Because sunlight can penetrate this zone, photosynthesis is possible. It is the warmest layer of the ocean and the richest in nutrients. Phytoplankton, which form the base of the food chain in many parts of the ocean, live here. The depth of this zone is variable; it depends on the turbidity of the water.

2

OLIGOPHOTIC

Extending to a depth of 1,600 feet (500 meters), this zone is also known as the penumbral zone. It receives enough light for animals to see during the day. It is the location where the constant struggle between predator and prey occurs.

TRIESTE

The bathyscaphe *Trieste* from the United States reached a depth of 35,810 feet (10,916 meters) in the Challenger Deep of the Marianas Trench. This record still stands.

Bioluminescence

Known as cold light, it is produced by a chemical reaction in specialized cells called photocytes that exist in certain organisms. The light that is produced is generally greenish-blue and can serve as a form of communication to attract potential mates, to frighten away other organisms, or as camouflage from enemies. This feature is very common among deep-ocean fish, squid, bacteria, and jellyfish. It is also found in various terrestrial organisms such as fireflies.

LUMINOUS LURE
The light attracts prey to the deep-sea predator.

HYDROSTATIC PRESSURE

The weight of the water column. It varies with water density and depth. During a descent, the hydrostatic pressure increases quickly.

3

APHOTIC
This zone can extend between 650 and 13,000 feet (200 and 4,000 meters), depending on the time of year and the turbidity of the water. There is too little sunlight for photosynthesis, and the resulting lack of food is the main problem for the animals that live at this depth.

4

ABYSSAL
Located between 13,000 and 26,000 feet (3,000 and 6,000 meters), this zone is characterized by cold conditions, a scarcity of nutrients, and total darkness. Some of the animals that live there are very large, and some have a monstrous appearance.

DEADLY JAW
This weapon helps this hunter survive 3,300 feet (1,000 meters) under water.

BEARD
This structure may also produce light for attracting prey.

DEEPSEA ANGLER
Linophryne arborifera
It has a luminous lure attached to its head and a branching beard that also gives off light to attract prey. The male is smaller than the female, and it lives off the female as a parasite.

5

HADAL
This very cold zone with very high hydrostatic pressure extends below 20,000 feet (6,000 meters). It is associated with deep-ocean trenches and accounts for less than 2% of the area of the ocean floor.

DIMENSIONS

WEIGHT
10.5 ounces (300 grams)

3.9 inches (10 cm)

IN DARKNESS

A few fish species live at depths below 8,200 feet (2,500 meters). They are known as abyssal fish, and they have peculiar facial features, such as large heads, sharp teeth, and photospheres that glow in the darkness.

The Seashore

A long both the rocky and sandy coasts, where the sea meets land, the movements of the tides outline well-defined habitats that are rich in wildlife. Certain areas are covered by water during high tide. When the tide goes out, these areas are exposed to the air. Organisms that live in this environment must be adapted to life both in and out of the water. Although the tidal zone differs from place to place, the shore is always divided into three zones: supralittoral, intertidal (or littoral), and infralittoral. ●

EURASIAN OYSTER-CATCHER
Haematopus ostralegus

TOMPOT BLENNY
Parablennius gattorugine

BEADLET ANEMONE
Actinia equina

SKELETON OF AN EDIBLE SEA URCHIN
Echinus esculentus

COMMON STARFISH
Asterias rubens

STRAWBERRY ANEMONE
Actinia fragacea

SUPRALITTORAL
Of the three zones, this one is farthest from the reach of the tide. It is not usually submerged, but it is affected by sea salt. It can become flooded every 15 days during a leap tide.

INTERTIDAL
This intermediate zone is alternately covered by water and exposed to the air.

SURVIVAL
The fish in the rocky pools are well camouflaged and swim very rapidly to avoid being caught. Starfish have an unusual ability to regenerate lost arms.

INFRALITTORAL This part of the shore is always below the water. It gradually transitions to the inner continental shelf. The border fluctuates; it is marked by the average wave height. Most of the animals that live in the infralittoral zone are completely marine, although some come out of the ocean to reproduce.

Life on the Seashore

The tides govern the life of the animals on the shore. Most have an internal biological clock, adjusted to the rhythm of the tides, and can anticipate tide-related events. Crabs, for example, come out to feed during low tide. Algae have filaments that they attach to rocks to prevent them from being carried out to sea. Starfish and sea urchins slowly crawl over rocky surfaces with hundreds of fluid-filled feet. One way living things can protect themselves from predators is by hiding under the sand. Buried clams have a tubelike part that extends to the sand's surface. Another species found under the sand, the lugworm, lives in burrows with small holes. Water enters and waste, resembling squeezed toothpaste, is discharged through the holes.

FOOD
The diversity of food found on the seashore is much greater than that in the open ocean.

Symbiotic Relationship

This type of relationship, common to many habitats, is especially evident along the coasts. Zooxanthella, microscopic algae that live inside the bodies of animals such as coral, are found in coastal waters. They create food for the coral through the process of photosynthesis. In return, they receive protection. The giant clam also lives on the nutrients produced by these algae; algae grows on the clam's thick lips.

GREAT SCALLOP
Pecten maximus

EUROPEAN PLAICE
Pleuronectes platessa

MOON JELLY
Aurelia aurita

CUTTLEFISH
Sepia officinalis

HAWAIIAN ZEBRA HERMIT CRAB
Calcinus laevimanus

Cementation

The process by which sediments are transformed into rock when they are joined with particles supplied by flowing water. When the water evaporates or cools, the dissolved minerals can precipitate. Deposits of material can accumulate and bond with other sediment or form rocks on their own. Sandstone is one example of rock formed through cementation.

RAG WORM
Neanthes virens

SNAKELOCKS ANEMONE
Anemonia viridis

Rocky Pool

Formed by the movement of the tides, these pools are often small, but they can also be large and deep. They are essentially miniature oceans that are home to a large variety of microorganisms, photosynthetic plants, and fish. Fish in these pools are generally small, fast, and well camouflaged. Other inhabitants include hermit crabs (which seek shelter inside the empty shells of dead mollusks) and dangerous sea anemones (which conceal deadly, paralyzing tentacles). Jellyfish, starfish, and mussels are also commonly found in rocky pools.

DUNGENESS CRAB
Cancer magister

Coral Reefs

Present for more than 450 million years, coral reefs sit beneath shallow, warm ocean waters between the Tropics of Cancer and Capricorn. Coral reefs are veritable rainforests of the sea; their biodiversity encompasses almost one-third of all ocean species. The reefs are solid structures composed primarily of coral rock formed from the calcium carbonate secreted by coral polyps. Many organisms contain very potent biochemical substances. ●

SEA ANEMONE *Actinia*
This solitary polyp has retractable, stinging tentacles used for defense and for the capture of prey. There are more than 800 species. Most live attached to rocky surfaces, although they can creep along the seabed.

CONSERVATION
Coral reefs can require many years to reach full size; they need at least 20 years to grow to the size of a soccer ball. Global warming is one of the major causes of the widespread deterioration of coral colonies. Other threats to coral reefs include tourism and pollution.

POWERFUL POISON
Despite its small size (less than 8 inches [20 cm]), this octopus is capable of killing a person. It releases extremely poisonous saliva into the water to stun and catch its prey, or it can inject the venom with a fatal bite. When it is disturbed, the iridescence of the rings on its skin glow more brightly. It is the most dangerous cephalopod.

CONTINUOUS BARRIER
This barrier reef is separated from the coast by saltwater lagoons. It is made up of colonies of coral polyps that secrete a hard exoskeleton of calcium carbonate. As the polyps divide and the colony grows, the reef becomes larger.

BLUE-RINGED OCTOPUS
Hapalochlaena maculosa

Types of Reefs

There are some 230,000 square miles (600,000 sq km) of coral reefs in the world's oceans. They were originally classified in 1842 by Charles Darwin, who described three principal types. Fringing, or coastal, reefs grow in shallow waters near the shoreline on the continental shelf. They support the most complex aquatic ecosystems. Barrier reefs, such as the Great Barrier Reef of Australia, are separated from continental landmasses by shallow saltwater lagoons that can become very wide and deep. Atolls, such as the Tahitian atoll, are ring-shaped. They surround a deep central lagoon, which is as rich in sealife as the coral reef itself. Atolls originate from fringing reefs that form around the sides of a volcanic island. Later, the volcano becomes submerged, either as a result of rising sea levels or because of the sinking of the volcanic island itself. The reefs continue to grow until only the ring of coral remains. Atolls are generally located far from continental landmasses.

Life in the Coral Reef

In addition to coral polyps, coral reefs house a large number of multicolored species (such as fish, tortoises, starfish, giant clams, snails, octopuses, sponges, tubular worms, sea urchins, anemones, and others). The inhabitants build a complex web of associations. Many animals can live together without competing for the same prey. The reef has countless small nooks that predators and prey use for shelter. Every food source in the reef is recycled through food chains. Food chains begin with diminutive single-celled algae that live inside the coral polyps. Algae also help to produce the limestone necessary for the construction of the reef.

BARRIER REEF
of Bora Bora in the Society Islands of French Polynesia

Symbiosis

This is a relationship between different organisms that live together in close association. In particular, mutualism is a type of symbiosis in which both organisms benefit. Although it is found in all habitats, symbiosis is especially prevalent in coastal areas of the ocean. A common example found in coral reefs is the clown fish, which lives among the tentacles of large sea anemones. It is protected from the anemone's stinging cells by a coating of mucous. While the anemone's stinging tentacles protect the fish from predators, the fish cleans the anemone by ingesting harmful material that collects on the anemone's outer covering.

LETHAL SPINE
This voracious predator attacks its prey by inflicting a painful wound with the venomous spines of its pectoral fins. It feeds on small shrimp and crabs as well as very large fish.

WHAT IS CORAL?
A piece of coral is the skeletal remains of microscopic animals. These animals are tubular polyps less than 0.3 inches (5 mm) in diameter. They affix themselves to a substrate by means of a hard basal disk. Each polyp has an opening that is connected to a gastric cavity that secretes the calcium carbonate substance that forms the reef. Coral can take many shapes; it can resemble such objects as trees, mushrooms, and flowers.

LIONFISH
Pterois volitans

CLOWN FISH
Amphiprion ocellaris

BARREL SPONGE
Xestospongia testudinaria

YELLOW-TUBED SPONGE
Aplysina fistularis

BLUE TUBE SPONGE
Kallypilidion fascigera

Freshwater Ecosystems

Although most of the water that evaporates from the oceans condenses and falls as rain or snow and later returns to the atmosphere, about one-third of it returns to the ocean as runoff from the land. On land, the water helps to create a variety of habitats: rivers, lakes, ponds, and wetlands. The animals in these habitats need to contend with conditions that range from strong currents to droughts. Some of the animals are not exclusively aquatic; they alternate between land and water. These animals enter the water to hunt, reproduce, or shelter their young. ●

Rivers and Lakes

Rivers form part of the water cycle, carrying water from rain or melted snow from higher elevations to lakes, ponds, or the ocean. Rivers are in constant motion and follow a course that can be divided into three main sections: upper, middle, and lower. As they flow, rivers can carry various types of matter with them and cause erosion. A single stretch of a river can have several types of currents and can pass through different soils. The dynamic characteristics of rivers contrast with the placid waters of lakes. Eventually, lakes will fill with sediment and disappear. The origin of many lakes is associated with glaciation, although tectonic movement and volcanic eruptions have also produced basins that fill with water to become lakes.

UPPER COURSE
Mountain terrain is rugged, and the river course is very steep, dropping at least 21 to 26 feet per mile (4 to 5 meters per km). The turbulent waters flow rapidly, typically more than 1.5 feet (0.5 meters) per second, and form rapids and waterfalls. Such areas typically have few people.

URBAN AREAS
The mouth of a major river is commonly where urban or industrial centers are located.

MIDDLE COURSE
In this section, the steepness and speed of the river, as well as its erosive power, decrease. The river channel widens, and water carries material eroded from higher stretches of the river. In the river's quiet pools live snails, leeches, dragonflies, and mosquitoes. Most of the fish here are herbivorous; they include barbs and gobies.

LOWER COURSE
The land is fairly flat, and the river water flows slowly. The river course meanders, creating large loops, and the river channel widens as it nears the mouth of the river. The impact of human activities is important here.

BROWN BEAR
Ursus arctos

Migrations

Rivers and lakes receive migrating fish that are able to switch between freshwater and saltwater environments. Most of these fish move between habitats in order to reproduce. For example, salmon leave the sea to reproduce in the safer habitat of a river, even if it requires swimming 1,500 miles (2,500 km) across an ocean. The lack of food in the rivers, however, drives young salmon down the river and back to the sea. Thanks to a well-developed sense of smell, the salmon at sea remember precisely where they were hatched and return to that specific location to spawn. In contrast, freshwater eels swim out to sea in order to reproduce. Along the way, eels sometimes slide over the open ground to avoid rapids and waterfalls; eels have a limited ability to breathe through their skin.

HUNTING IN THE WATER
Coastal populations of brown bears can spend hours in shallow river courses waiting to catch—with the help of their large paws—protein-rich salmon. Every year, salmon swim upriver to spawn.

On the Bank of a Tropical River

The margins of the Amazon River shelter animals of the rainforest, including small but feared predators such as piranhas (carnivorous fish with sharp slashing teeth that can finish off a tapir within minutes), anacondas (the longest snakes in the world, which eat their prey whole), and arawanas (fish that can jump almost 3 feet [1 meter] out of the water to capture insects sitting on the thick foliage along the river's edge). Other species include monkeys (such as the spider monkey and red howler money), deer, and capybara (a semiaquatic rodent). Many birds (such as the green-billed toucan, hoatzin, scarlet ibis, and jacamar) are also found here.

SHARED SPACE

Using its long curved beak, the scarlet ibis can dig into the mud for its food. Its diet includes mollusks, insects, fish, amphibians, seeds, fruits, and crustaceans. By eating crustaceans, such as shrimp, the bird receives its characteristic color. By sharing its feeding areas with other wading birds (such as storks and roseate spoonbills), it can better avoid predators.

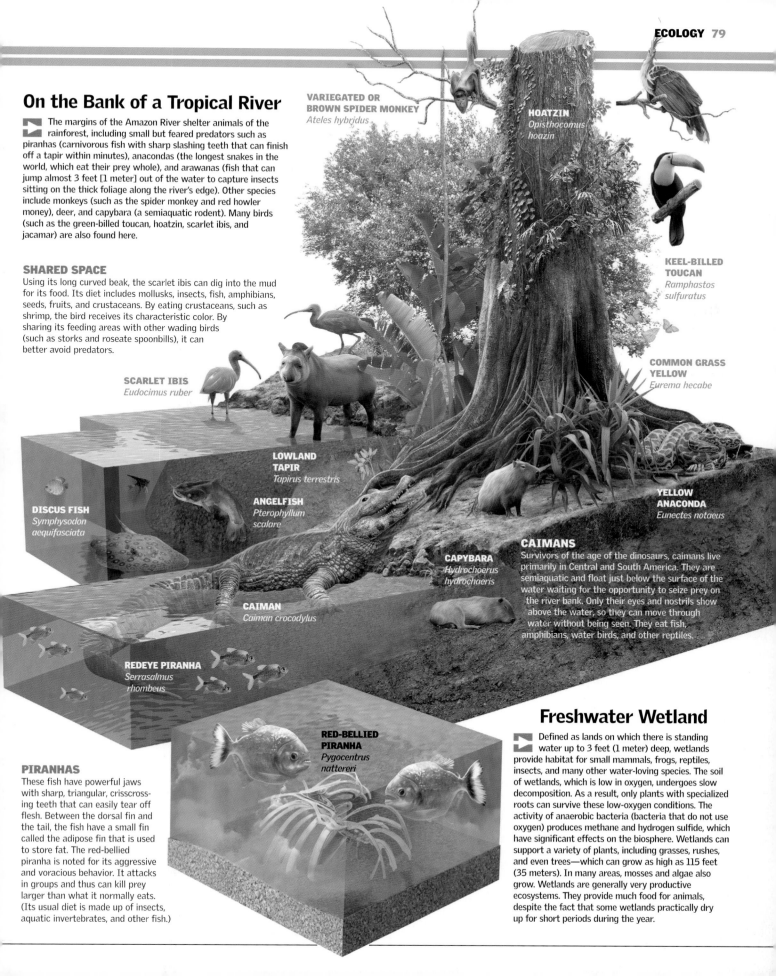

VARIEGATED OR BROWN SPIDER MONKEY
Ateles hybridus

HOATZIN
Opisthocomus hoazin

KEEL-BILLED TOUCAN
Ramphastos sulfuratus

COMMON GRASS YELLOW
Eurema hecabe

SCARLET IBIS
Eudocimus ruber

LOWLAND TAPIR
Tapirus terrestris

ANGELFISH
Pterophyllum scalare

YELLOW ANACONDA
Eunectes notaeus

DISCUS FISH
Symphysodon aequifasciata

CAIMAN
Caiman crocodylus

CAPYBARA
Hydrochoerus hydrochaeris

REDEYE PIRANHA
Serrasalmus rhombeus

RED-BELLIED PIRANHA
Pygocentrus nattereri

CAIMANS

Survivors of the age of the dinosaurs, caimans live primarily in Central and South America. They are semiaquatic and float just below the surface of the water waiting for the opportunity to seize prey on the river bank. Only their eyes and nostrils show above the water, so they can move through water without being seen. They eat fish, amphibians, water birds, and other reptiles.

PIRANHAS

These fish have powerful jaws with sharp, triangular, crisscrossing teeth that can easily tear off flesh. Between the dorsal fin and the tail, the fish have a small fin called the adipose fin that is used to store fat. The red-bellied piranha is noted for its aggressive and voracious behavior. It attacks in groups and thus can kill prey larger than what it normally eats. (Its usual diet is made up of insects, aquatic invertebrates, and other fish.)

Freshwater Wetland

Defined as lands on which there is standing water up to 3 feet (1 meter) deep, wetlands provide habitat for small mammals, frogs, reptiles, insects, and many other water-loving species. The soil of wetlands, which is low in oxygen, undergoes slow decomposition. As a result, only plants with specialized roots can survive these low-oxygen conditions. The activity of anaerobic bacteria (bacteria that do not use oxygen) produces methane and hydrogen sulfide, which have significant effects on the biosphere. Wetlands can support a variety of plants, including grasses, rushes, and even trees—which can grow as high as 115 feet (35 meters). In many areas, mosses and algae also grow. Wetlands are generally very productive ecosystems. They provide much food for animals, despite the fact that some wetlands practically dry up for short periods during the year.

Small Lakes and Ponds

Smaller and shallower than lakes, these bodies of standing water range from 6.5 to 100 feet (2 to 30 meters) deep. These conditions are adequate for harboring a rich, diverse habitat made up primarily of various types of aquatic plants and animals. Several organisms (such as snails, frogs, newts, fish, insects, and even ducks) can live both in and out of the water. The amount of dissolved oxygen in the water can vary enormously during the course of the day. The water temperature varies seasonally, and this helps to determine the fauna and flora. During the summer, the temperature can vary from 39° F (4° C) near the bottom to 72° F (22° C) at the surface. In winter, the temperature can be 39° F (4° C) near the bottom and only 32° F (0° C) near the surface. In extremely cold regions, it is possible for all the water in the pond to freeze.

EGGS
The common frog lays its eggs in a cluster that floats just below the surface of the water. When these clusters are combined, they form a large mass.

MALLARD
Anas platyrhynchos
This duck species can adjust to all types of aquatic habitats. When it feeds, it often adopts a vertical position to reach submerged plants and invertebrates.

MARSH FROG
Rana ridibunda
This is the largest frog in Europe. Its croak is one of the most varied among all the amphibians of Europe. Marsh frogs sing together during the day and at night in both spring and summer. Singing is especially pronounced during mating season. The marsh frog hibernates in water, in bottom mud or in burrows along the shore. It has a relatively large head, and its powerful hind legs make it an excellent jumper. The frog is edible and is particularly prized in French cuisine.

4,000
the number of eggs that a female frog lays at one time, covered in a protective gelatinous substance

Photic Zone
Unlike lakes, which are typically more than 100 feet (30 meters) deep, small lakes and ponds are shallow enough that sunlight can reach all areas of the bottom substrate. Photosynthesis can therefore take place throughout a small lake or pond. Plants can grow anywhere within such a habitat. The function of the photic zone is crucial ecologically. Photosynthetic organisms, such as cyanobacteria and algae, transform energy from the Sun into organic matter in the photic zone. This matter is consumed by the rest of the organisms in the food chain.

EELGRASS
Vallisneria spiralis

Green Algae
These photosynthetic organisms are neither plants nor animals. They can be unicellular, like diatoms, or multicellular. Green algae constitute the most common species in an aquatic environment. One example is Spirogyra, which appears as a tangle of thousands of pale green hairlike filaments. It proliferates in the spring and can completely cover the water's surface, depriving other plants in the water of sunlight. Most species of green algae are benthic (that is, attached to the bottom), but there are planktonic species that live suspended in the water. The algae release oxygen as they produce food, thereby increasing the amount of dissolved oxygen in the water. Its overgrowth, however, which commonly occurs during the summer, can cause the death of many plants and animals.

NORTHERN PIKE
Esox lucius
This voracious and opportunistic predator, camouflaged with light-colored markings, is characterized by having a single dorsal fin. It approaches its prey by rippling the surface of the water. It uses the subaquatic vegetation to lie in wait for prey.

Aquatic Plants

The presence of these plants in this habitat is very important as a source of food, oxygen, and shelter. Most of the food is produced by minuscule organisms such as *Volvox* (a type of green algae) that make up the base of the food chain. The large variety of plants is subdivided into specific zones. For example, amphibious plants (such as bulrushes, reeds, and arrowhead) and aquatic plants (such as eelgrass) grow near the shore. Farther from shore, in open water, only aquatic plants grow. Floating plants, such as duckweed and aquatic ferns, have small, unattached roots. These roots can absorb nutrients directly from the water, in contrast with submerged plants, such as Elodea, which send their roots into the mud at the bottom to obtain nutrients.

PLANKTON Near the surface, both phytoplankton and zooplankton form the base of the food chain.

RED-SIDED GARTER SNAKE
Thamnophis sirtalis parietalis

This species of garter snake hibernates during the winter, because of both the season's low temperatures and the few hours available for sunning. It is capable of traveling 2.5 miles (4 km) in search of a place to hibernate, where it joins hundreds of other snakes. Mating typically takes place at this time, and individuals can locate each other by tracking their pheromones. The snake is carnivorous and swallows its prey whole.

LAKE ZONES

Sunlight is quickly absorbed both by water and by microorganisms. The absorption of light divides the lake into two horizontal layers (photic and aphotic).

The depth of these layers is affected by variations in light and temperature. The photic layer is subdivided into the littoral and limnetic zones.

FRESHWATER TURTLES
The turtles that live in fresh water, unlike terrestrial turtles, are primarily carnivorous. Freshwater turtles have other distinctive traits, such as leatherlike skin under their shells.

BENTHIC ZONE The bottom of the lake. This zone is covered with mud and serves as an area of decomposition, where organisms such as anaerobic bacteria grow.

CHINESE SOFT-SHELLED TURTLE
Pelodiscus sinensis
This turtle, which has webbed feet for swimming, can breathe below the water's surface thanks to its long snout and tubelike nose. It rests on the bottom of bodies of water covered with sand or mud. It can also bite aggressively when threatened.

LITTORAL ZONE Adjacent to the shore, with rooted and floating plants. This zone contains variable fauna such as snakes, insects, crustaceans, fish, and amphibians.

LIMNETIC ZONE Open area away from shore. This zone is characterized by phytoplankton and the small fish that feed on it.

APHOTIC ZONE The underwater area that is not exposed to sunlight. In this zone, organisms cannot carry out photosynthesis; however, the mineralization of nutrients can occur here.

COLORFUL WARNING
The bright coloration typical of newts can serve as camouflage or as a warning to predators. Bright colors often indicate an animal's ability to produce toxic substances.

340
MILLION YEARS
the length of time amphibians have lived on the planet

ORIENTAL FIRE-BELLIED NEWT
Cynops orientalis
This Chinese salamander secretes mildly toxic poisons through its skin. Nevertheless, it is in demand as a pet.

Humans and the Biosphere

Humans are not ordinary living beings. For the first time in Earth's history, a species is capable of causing global effects through its activities. Humans are changing the balance of nature; however, they are also a part of nature. How do humans affect the biosphere? The darker side of humanity is revealed in how it treats the environment. On the other hand, the

COAL MINING
is one of the most hazardous jobs in the world. Explosions, cave-ins, collisions, mechanical accidents, equipment safety failures, and dust pollution cause irreparable harm to health.

thousands of ways in which humans study living things and humanity's efforts across the globe to live harmoniously with the rest of the planet's inhabitants is most encouraging. Throughout human history, people have been concerned with protecting the environment and saving resources for the future. Since the 1990s, several far-reaching international environmental conventions and treaties have met with success. ●

The Scope of Human Activity

O f the five billion years of Earth's history, humans have existed for only the past 100,000 years—a tiny fraction. Their presence, however, has set off dramatic changes in the biosphere. For the first time, a single species exercises total supremacy over the rest and carries out activities that have global implications. This species has even developed the means to destroy much of the life on the planet. The changes are serious and without precedent; their long-term consequences are difficult to predict. ●

Demographic Explosion

➤ Until the 18th century, the world population grew at a steady pace. During the agricultural and industrial revolutions, however, humans acquired new technology that increased the availability of resources. New technologies, together with advances in medicine, led to exponential human population growth.

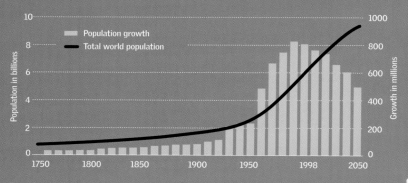

Legend:
- Population growth
- Total world population

Left axis: Population in billions (0, 2, 4, 6, 8, 10)
Right axis: Growth in millions (0, 200, 400, 600, 800, 1000)
X axis: 1750, 1800, 1850, 1900, 1950, 1998, 2050

From the graph, it can be seen that the rate of fertility appears to be decreasing, despite enormous population growth. Some authorities predict that the human population will stabilize in about 2100, at which point there will be about 10.5 billion persons on the planet.

Profound Effects

➤ Many human activities have impacts that are not restricted to limited areas. Unlike other species, human activities can be recorded on a global scale.

HEAT ISLAND

Industrial emissions, toxic spills, herbicides, and fertilizers have, over the past centuries, introduced large amounts of pollutants into the air, water, and soil. In some cases, they have caused significant harm and disruption to Earth's fauna and flora.

The concentration of greenhouse gases from AD 1 to 2005

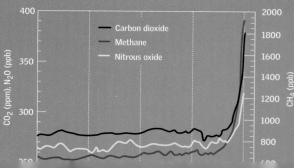

Legend:
- Carbon dioxide
- Methane
- Nitrous oxide

Left axis: CO_2 (ppm), N_2O (ppb) (250, 300, 350, 400)
Right axis: CH_4 (ppb) (600, 800, 1000, 1200, 1400, 1600, 1800, 2000)

630 billion

The number of human beings who would exist in 2060, if the population were to continue multiplying at the rate that it has since the 18th century. This means that there would not be more than 0.5 square inch (3 sq cm) of space available for each person on the planet.

2,700 square miles (7,000 sq km)

The loss of rainforest in the Amazon in only eight months between August and December 2007. This figure raised alarms concerning the indiscriminate logging of the planet's "green lung."

93%

The percentage of temperate forest in Madagascar—the most seriously eroded country in the world—that has been cut down. (66% of its rainforest has suffered the same fate.)

35%

The percentage of the total land area that is desert.

DESERTIFICATION

Indiscriminate logging, population growth, and intensive agriculture have turned formerly fertile areas into deserts. The map shows, in red, the regions most vulnerable to desertification.

Vulnerability
- Low
- Moderate
- High
- Very High

Other Regions
- Dry
- Cold
- Humid/Not Vulnerable

LOSS OF BIODIVERSITY

In some cases, the intensive exploitation of a species leaves it at the edge of extinction. In others, the loss of habitat is what leads to a species' disappearance.

ACID RAIN

Industrial emissions, especially those that contain sulfur and nitrogen, lead to acidic rain and other forms of precipitation containing pollutants that have a profound impact on ecosystems, particularly in the Northern Hemisphere.

CLIMATE CHANGE

The average near-surface global temperature of the Earth is increasing. Researchers continue to investigate the extent to which the carbon dioxide produced through human activity contributes to this increase.

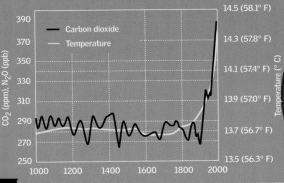

Legend (chart):
— Carbon dioxide
— Temperature

Left axis: CO_2 (ppm), N_2O (ppb): 250, 270, 290, 310, 330, 350, 370, 390

Right axis: Temperature (° C): 13.5 (56.3° F), 13.7 (56.7° F), 13.9 (57.0° F), 14.1 (57.4° F), 14.3 (57.8° F), 14.5 (58.1° F)

X axis: 1000, 1200, 1400, 1600, 1800, 2000

THE OZONE HOLE

The annual thinning of the ozone layer, the part of the atmosphere that protects the Earth's surface from the bulk of harmful incoming ultraviolet radiation, might be the result of human activity.

The Urban Ecosystem

The agglomerations of roads and buildings in which hundreds of thousands to millions of persons coexist produce major changes to the landscape. Urban areas can even modify the local climate. The presence of urban areas does not mean, however, that fauna and flora disappear. On the contrary, even though some native animals and plants may completely die off, other species manage to adapt to urban areas. Often, these species are the ones that find it impossible to live away from people. ●

Urban Microclimate

The microclimate of cities has characteristic properties that result from the massive concentration of concrete. Urban areas often lack green spaces, and their microclimates are driven by the gaseous emissions from factories, automobiles, and other by-products of human industry, such as pollution.

HEAT ISLAND

The temperature in large cities is, on average, 2.7° F (1.5° C) warmer than in the surrounding area. When the temperature falls at night, the concrete from roads and buildings radiates some of the heat it absorbed during the day. This temperature difference between cities and surrounding areas can be as great as 9° F (5° C).

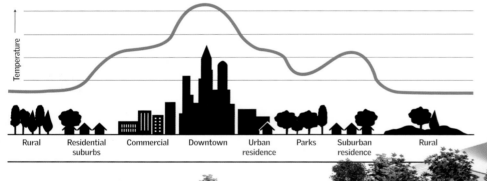

| Rural | Residential suburbs | Commercial | Downtown | Urban residence | Parks | Suburban residence | Rural |

Temperature (y-axis)

HUMIDITY

It tends to be lower, although rainfall is heavier and more plentiful.

SOLAR RADIATION

It is between 15 and 20% less, because the sky is usually dimmed by particulate matter, carbon dioxide, and water vapor.

WINDS

Structures create concrete barriers that reduce wind strength by 20%.

AIR QUALITY

The air in cities contains large amounts of pollution and particulate matter.

World of Concrete

Concrete and polluted city air provide ideal conditions for some species; however, others are only relatively successful in this unnatural environment. Some species (such as rats and cockroaches) adapt so well to city life that they become a nuisance to people.

Parks and plazas

In cities, these areas contain the greatest biodiversity. Native species coexist with introduced species. Migratory birds even use these places for stopovers.

1.2 billion acres
(480 million hectares)

The total area occupied by all the great urban centers of the world. This is equivalent to 4% of the planet's surface area.

High Above

Birds and bats make nests on roofs and on window ledges. Other animals (such as insects and rodents) use buildings as living spaces, reaching altitudes that they would never be able to reach in nature.

Sterile concrete?

Concrete does not stop the march of life. Several kinds of plants can grow from cracks or holes in the pavement. Plants also use the water that collects in these spaces. The plants can, in turn, provide a home for numerous microorganisms.

Survival Strategies

The city presents advantages for numerous species. Its climate is more stable, and there are no large predators. It is a complex environment, however, and it requires a number of strategies to be able to survive.

FLEXIBLE DIET

Many species adopt new eating habits. In many cases, their diet is based on the garbage discarded by people.

HUMAN CONTACT

Many species lose their fear of people as they come in contact with them. The minimum safe distance between humans and animals shrinks, and some animals (such as pigeons) even establish physical contact.

LEARNING NEW BEHAVIORS

Animals learn how to tear open bags of garbage and steal food. Cases have been reported in which birds (the blue tit, *Parus caeruleus*) have opened bottles of milk in Great Britain.

LOWER DENSITY, BETTER SURVIVAL

Although it would appear that the density of a given population of animals is less in the urban environment than in the wild, each individual animal is able to live longer in general.

Champions at Adaptation

Some species have adjusted so magnificently to urban life that they form a part of the urban landscape in almost all cities around the world.

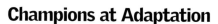

PIGEONS AND SPARROWS

These birds are present in all major urban centers. They nest in the city's trees or buildings and incorporate garbage into their diets.

BATS

These mammals nest in high places. Although feared for their appearance and nocturnal habits, they help control bothersome populations of mosquitoes.

RATS

They can live underground and eat cockroaches and garbage.

SPIDERS

A large number of species have adapted to urban life. Some even build their nests inside houses. They feed on insects.

COCKROACHES, ANTS, AND MOTHS

They have adjusted extremely well to living in cities with people. They are practically impossible to eradicate.

MOSQUITOES

Not only do they live alongside human beings, but the females even feed on human blood in order to reproduce.

Below Ground

This region is inhabited by significant colonies of insects and rats, which come out at night to find food. In addition, underground areas contain a variety of fungi, bacteria, and worms.

280

The number of offspring that a single female rat produces in its lifetime. The female can become fertile just 48 hours after giving birth.

The Study of Nature

Unraveling the most complex secrets of nature is an arduous task that sometimes takes many years of research and more than one generation of scientists. All serious scientific inquiry is based on the scientific method, and in the case of ecology, it usually involves theoretical components (the formulation of a hypothesis and conclusions) and practical considerations (performing field research). There are a series of tools and special methods that scientists use to study living organisms. ●

The Scientific Method

To establish verifiable knowledge, the scientific method is used. The "truths" obtained by this method should be verifiable, and the experiments should be reproducible by anyone.

1 HYPOTHESIS

It is a provisional explanation drawn from early observations. It needs to be tested through experimentation.

22 years

The length of time naturalist Charles Darwin delayed in publishing *On the Origin of Species*, the theory he used to explain evolution through the mechanism of natural selection.

5 CONCLUSION

Conclusions are based on results and interpretation of collected data. A conclusion might show that the hypothesis was false. In many cases, a false hypothesis serves as the starting point for new hypotheses that can be put to the test. Of course, the results of an experiment can also confirm the initial hypothesis. In these cases, the experiment should be repeatable, so that other scientists can confirm the work.

A scientific work is validated once it is published in a peer-reviewed journal.

6,000

The number of living blue whales *(Balaenoptera musculus),* the largest animal in the world

4 ANALYSIS OF DATA

The data that have been obtained are processed and analyzed.

Taking Samples

In accordance with the area of study, ecologists use various methods to take field samples.

SQUARES, TRANSECTS, AND NETS

Because it is often impossible to count every specimen in an entire region, square plots are used. A count of the species within the plot is made, and that information is then extrapolated for the entire region.

Transects, on the other hand, are typically used in areas where there are variations and transitions of organism types. In this technique, the researcher counts individuals while following a straight line through the study area. An attempt is made to link the results with the variations in the environment.

Nets are effective tools for capturing insects, plankton, fish, and even birds.

TAGGING

For some studies, it is necessary to tag animals and then release them. Satellite technology makes large-scale tracking possible, although it requires the use of radio transmitters.

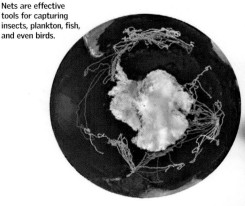

The satellite image shows the continent of Antarctica. The colored lines indicate the paths followed by different southern elephant seals (*Mirounga leonina*) tagged with radio transmitters.

2 **EXPERIMENT DESIGN**
Once the hypothesis has been established, experiments must be developed to test whether the explanation is valid or not.

4,900 feet (1,500 meters)

The depth to which elephant seals can dive. This fact was discovered thanks to studies using tracking transmitters.

TRAPS

There are countless traps for catching different types of animals. The picture shows a trap for night insects that are drawn to light.

The light attracts the insects.

An opaque cylinder has a screen at the bottom.

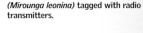

The funnel directs an insect toward the jar.

3 **EXPERIMENTS**
The experiments are carried out to test the hypothesis. In ecology, tests are usually related to samples collected from the field. Several methods are used, depending on the object of the study.

The jar contains a chemical to immobilize the insects.

0.003 inch (0.076 mm)

The size of the openings in the nets used to collect plankton

ANALYSIS OF THE ENVIRONMENT

In order to understand the life in any given location, it is necessary to study the area's climate, soil, and water.

Sustainable Solutions

I f the current trends of human activities continue, only a small fraction of wildlife will remain within a few decades, and the survival of human beings will be at risk. There are, however, some promising signs. In recent years, there has been a growing awareness of the ecological damage caused by human activities. Worldwide, many people are trying to find solutions to environmental problems, so that people can coexist harmoniously with their environment. ●

At the Top of the Agenda

As humans find solutions to counter the damage to the biosphere, certain steps should be taken immediately to produce the maximum benefit.

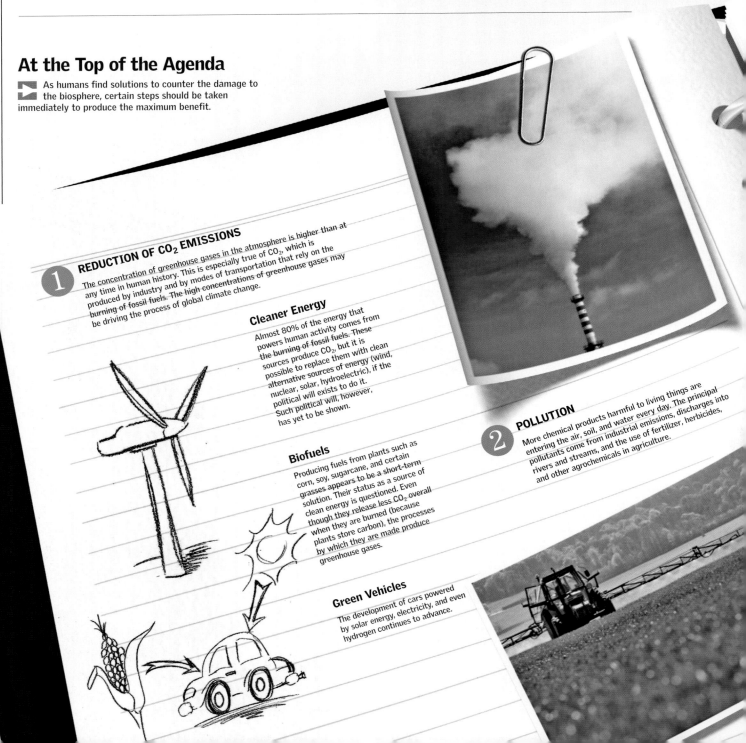

1 REDUCTION OF CO_2 EMISSIONS

The concentration of greenhouse gases in the atmosphere is higher than at any time in human history. This is especially true of CO_2, which is produced by industry and by modes of transportation that rely on the burning of fossil fuels. The high concentrations of greenhouse gases may be driving the process of global climate change.

Cleaner Energy

Almost 80% of the energy that powers human activity comes from the burning of fossil fuels. These sources produce CO_2, but it is possible to replace them with clean alternative sources of energy (wind, nuclear, solar, hydroelectric), if the political will exists to do it. Such political will, however, has yet to be shown.

Biofuels

Producing fuels from plants such as corn, soy, sugarcane, and certain grasses appears to be a short-term solution. Their status as a source of clean energy is questioned. Even though they release less CO_2 overall when they are burned (because plants store carbon), the processes by which they are made produce greenhouse gases.

Green Vehicles

The development of cars powered by solar energy, electricity, and even hydrogen continues to advance.

2 POLLUTION

More chemical products harmful to living things are entering the air, soil, and water every day. The principal pollutants come from industrial emissions, discharges into rivers and streams, and the use of fertilizer, herbicides, and other agrochemicals in agriculture.

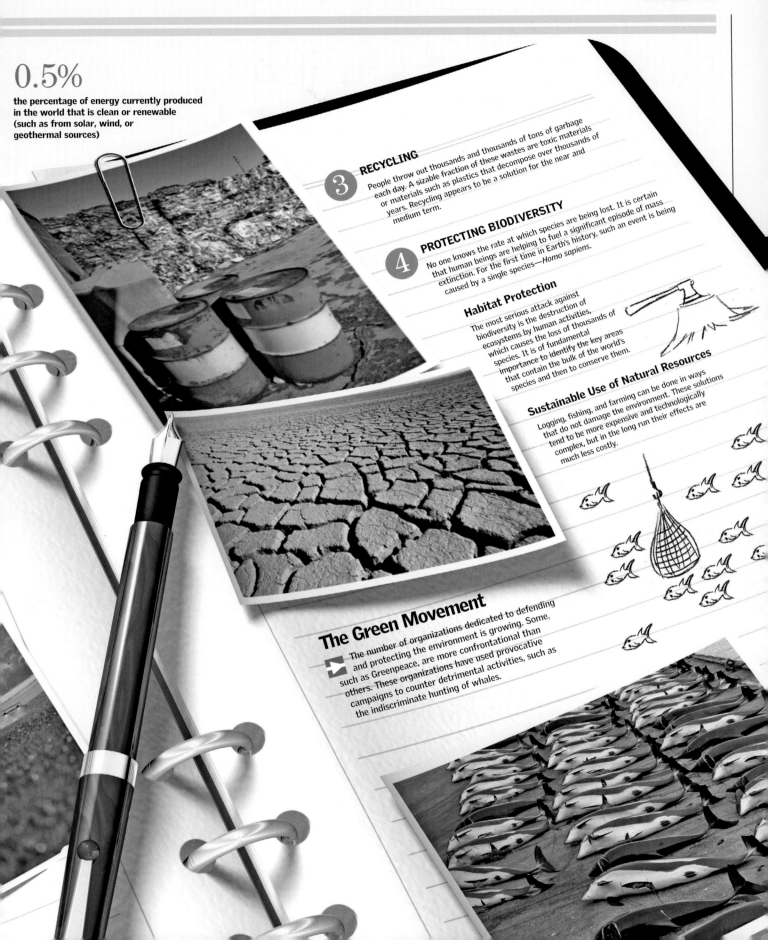

0.5%

the percentage of energy currently produced in the world that is clean or renewable (such as from solar, wind, or geothermal sources)

3 RECYCLING

People throw out thousands and thousands of tons of garbage each day. A sizable fraction of these wastes are toxic materials or materials such as plastics that decompose over thousands of years. Recycling appears to be a solution for the near and medium term.

4 PROTECTING BIODIVERSITY

No one knows the rate at which species are being lost. It is certain that human beings are helping to fuel a significant episode of mass extinction. For the first time in Earth's history, such an event is being caused by a single species—*Homo sapiens*.

Habitat Protection

The most serious attack against biodiversity is the destruction of ecosystems by human activities, which causes the loss of thousands of species. It is of fundamental importance to identify the key areas that contain the bulk of the world's species and then to conserve them.

Sustainable Use of Natural Resources

Logging, fishing, and farming can be done in ways that do not damage the environment. These solutions tend to be more expensive and technologically complex, but in the long run their effects are much less costly.

The Green Movement

The number of organizations dedicated to defending and protecting the environment is growing. Some, such as Greenpeace, are more confrontational than others. These organizations have used provocative campaigns to counter detrimental activities, such as the indiscriminate hunting of whales.

Glossary

Abyssal Zone

The ocean layer at a depth between 10,000 and 20,000 feet (3,000 and 6,000 meters), with low temperatures, a shortage of nutrients, and a total absence of light.

Acidity

The level of hydrogen concentration in soil. This is expressed as a pH (hydrogen potential) magnitude scale ranging from 0 to 14, where the lower the value, the greater the soil acidity, and the greater the value, the more alkaline the soil.

Anaerobic Bacteria

A type of bacteria that does not require oxygen to live; in fact, for some, it can even be lethal. Some of these bacteria grow in poorly-oxygenated areas of an organism and in tissues in the process of degenerating, such as in deep and dirty wounds, which can lead to infections.

Aphotic Zone

The layer of an ocean or a lake where no sunlight reaches and where photosynthesis cannot therefore occur.

Atoll

An island or group of several small oceanic coral islands in the form of a ring, with an interior lagoon that connects with the ocean.

Autochthonous Species

A species originating in a given area or that arrived there naturally and has remained for a significant period of time on the evolutionary scale.

Bedrock

The solid substrate that supports the soil, which forms the R horizon. Change in it from the effect of interaction with the atmosphere and living beings is the beginning of soil formation.

Benthic Zone

In a lake, the deepest layer, covered with mud, where the benthos live. In the ocean, the area that includes only the ocean floor.

Benthos

Organisms, such as certain plants, microorganisms, algae, bacteria, animals such as sponges, and some mollusks, that live at the bottom of aquatic environments.

Binomial Nomenclature

The convention used to scientifically name living beings through the combination of two words in Latin or from a Greco-Latin root; the first indicates the genus, and the second is a descriptor that completes the first to form the name of the species.

Biocenosis

A community of organisms coexisting in a biotope.

Biodiversity

The totality of the diverse species of living beings existing on the planet. In ecology, this concept also encompasses genetic differences within the same species and the diversity of ecosystems.

Biome

A group of ecosystems that shares a similar environment of vegetation and fauna. Terrestrial biomes are defined on the basis of the predominant vegetation and are grouped in forests (temperate, tropical, and boreal), grasslands, mountains, deserts, and polar regions, whereas the definition of aquatic biomes (sea and freshwater) is based on biogeochemical properties.

Biosphere

The space of the Earth where life occurs, which includes the surface layer of the planet, the hydrosphere, and the innermost layer of the atmosphere. This habitable region of the planet does not exceed 12 and a half miles (20 km) in thickness.

Biotope

The natural and limited physical space where a community of distinct animal and plant species develops.

Browser

An animal that feeds primarily off leaves, shoots, and fruits.

Camouflage

The ability of certain living beings to mimic their surroundings, so as to go unnoticed.

Canopy

The upper stratum or layer of the forest, formed by the crowns of the dominant trees.

Cellulose

A carbohydrate polymer present in the walls of plant cells, which is especially abundant in grass. Because it is difficult to digest, herbivores have microorganisms in their digestive systems capable of breaking cellulose down into absorbable components.

Cementation

The process through which sediments are transformed into rocks as particles brought by moving fluids become unified.

Colony

A group of living beings that live in close association, organized on a cooperative basis.

Commensalism

The symbiotic relationship between two species where one of them benefits, without harming or benefiting the other.

Community

A group of populations of distinct species of living beings that share a common environment and interact among themselves.

Competition

The condition existing between species of a community when they fight to obtain the same scarce resources. If competition occurs between two species, the stronger one generally ends up dominating, and the other becomes extinct.

Conifer

A tree or shrub whose seeds are produced in reproductive structures called cones. They are very resistant and are capable of surviving at low temperatures and with high winds. They are found in high latitudes as well as in high mountains in middle and tropical latitudes.

Coniferous Forest

A forest that is made up of species of conifers. It is characterized by low temperatures and by its density. It has soil with a high acidity index.

Consumer

In the trophic chain, a species that obtains its energy from living organisms or those that have recently died. Herbivores are primary consumers; carnivores that obtain their energy from herbivores are secondary consumers; these, in turn, are the source of energy for tertiary consumers; and so on.

Cooperation

The relationship between two species that share the same habitat and act in a complementary fashion without competing against each other for natural resources.

Coral

A small marine polyp, belonging to the Cnidaria phylum, which generates a calcareous skeleton. Corals group by the thousands and live in symbiosis with unicellular algae, forming colonies.

Coral Reef

The solid biological structure that develops in tropical waters near the shore and in shallow regions formed by the cementation of calcareous skeletons produced by colonies of polyps.

Deciduous Forest

A temperate forest, generally in the Northern Hemisphere, made up of deciduous tree species, that is, trees that lose their leaves in a given season of the year. Its soil is characterized by its rich layer of decomposing matter that favors the existence of numerous invertebrates.

Decomposer

An organism in the trophic chain that consumes dead organic matter. Fungi, bacteria, earthworms, among others, are decomposers.

Desert

Terrestrial biome characterized by extremely dry climate (less than 6 inches [15 cm] of precipitation per year), with great temperature variations between day and night and with scarce vegetation, consisting mainly of cactus and succulents. The fauna that live in it are especially adapted to economize water.

Ecological Niche

The total environment of a species, which includes the physical conditions (temperature, humidity, light . . .) and biological conditions (food, predators, competitors . . .) appropriate for its development and behavior.

Ecology

The science that studies the interactions among living beings and between those beings and their environment. The term was introduced in 1866 by Ernsz Haeckel, and it comes from the Greek terms *oikos* (home) and *logos* (knowledge).

Ecosystem

The unit formed by the entirety of populations that make up a community (living beings or biotic components) and the environment in which they develop (physical environment or abiotic components). The concept, developed beginning in the decade of the 1920s, takes into account the interactions of organisms among themselves, and with the environment, and the flows of energy and materials that take place in it.

Emergent Layer

The upper stratum of a tropical forest, above the canopy, made up of the crowns of isolated giant trees, which can reach 250 feet (75 m) in height.

Endemic Species

A unique biological species that lives in a defined geographic environment and that cannot be found naturally outside of that delimited area.

Epiphyte

An air plant that uses the trunk and/or branches of another plant as a support, rooting itself on it but without parasitizing it.

Evergreen Forest

A temperate forest made up of species of evergreen trees, that is, trees that maintain foliage throughout the year. It has abundant fauna at ground level.

Exclusion Principle

The principle by which, when two species enter into direct competition for the same limited resource, the winner survives and the loser becomes extinct.

Food, or Trophic, Chain

The entirety of chains or relations among the living beings of an ecosystem in relation to their nutrition and through which energy transfer occurs.

Grasslands

A great open expanse where pasturelands predominate and which can be found in temperate as well as tropical climates.

Gregarization

The tendency of certain animal species to group together permanently or temporarily.

Habitat

The physical place that provides the conditions for a species to live and to which it has adapted.

Hadal Zone

The oceanic layer below 20,000 feet (6,000 meters), with very low temperatures and great hydrostatic pressure.

Heat Island

The heat accumulation that occurs in urban areas as a consequence of the difficulty of dissipating heat at night. This situation is, in large measure, a result of the concentration of large amounts of heat-absorbing materials that, as the outside temperature falls during the night, release their heat into the atmosphere.

Horizon

The layer of soil parallel to the surface with specific characteristics resulting from the action of soil formation processes. Its structure, composition, and thickness depend on the type of minerals, climate, and living beings that helped in its formation and on the time elapsed.

Humus

A substance originating from the decomposition of organic matter in surface-layer soil. It contains a large amount of carbon, thus its blackish color.

Hydrothermal Vent

A fissure in volcanic regions of the ocean floor from which streams of very hot water and gases gush out at a temperature fluctuating between 270 and 400° C.

Infralittoral

The marine littoral zone that is always under water.

Kingdom

Each of the five groups (Animalia, Protista, Plantae, Prokaryota, and Fungi) in which living beings are classified, according to their morphological characteristics and their evolutionary history. It is the largest taxonomic category for organisms.

Lagoon

A natural deposit of stagnant water smaller than a lake, whose depth varies from 6 to 98 feet (2 to 30 meters). It is the habitat of numerous animal and plant species.

Limnetic Zone

Part of the (surficial) photic zone of a lake, far from the shore where phytoplankton live.

Littoral

Along the coast, the zone between the water and the supralittoral, which is submerged at high tide and exposed to the air at low tide. In lakes, it is the part of the photic zone from the edge of the water to the boundary of aquatic plants.

Marking

The system by which an animal under study is marked, so that once released it can be tracked.

Metabolic Water

The water produced by cell respiration from chemical reactions as energy is released from food. It is essential for animals that live in habitats where water is scarce.

Microclimate

A local climate of different characteristics from the area in which it is found.

Migration

The movement, usually seasonal, of certain species to other habitats in search of food or a warmer climate or to reproduce. Migration may be vertical (from higher altitude regions to lower ones) or horizontal (toward regions in other latitudes).

Mountain

In ecology, a terrestrial biome characterized by variability of temperature, amount of oxygen, and incidence of solar radiation as altitude increases. Present in different regions of the planet, it may be temperate or tropical.

Mutualism

The symbiotic relationship between two species from which both benefit.

Ocean Trench

A depression in the ocean floor several kilometers deep, created when oceanic plates collide.

Oligophotic Zone

The ocean layer immediately below the photic, which can extend to a depth of 1,500 feet (500 meters). Little light penetrates, but enough for animals to see during the day.

Parasitism

The symbiotic relationship between two species, in which one of them benefits and the other is harmed.

Pastureland

Terrain where grass abounds.

Permafrost

The layer of frozen soil perennially present in the polar regions and tundra and in a discontinuous manner any place in the world with average temperatures below 0° C.

Photic Zone

The surface layer of an ocean or a freshwater body, warm and rich in nutrients, where phytoplankton grow.

Phytoplankton

The aggregate of aquatic living beings of plant origin (microscopic organisms and unicellular algae) with the ability to carry out photosynthesis and that float freely. Phytoplankton is located in the layer of the oceans closest to the surface and is the base of the ocean food chain.

Population

A group of individuals of the same species that inhabit a given area and that are capable of reproducing with one another.

Population Density

The number of individuals per surface unit area.

Predation

The eating of living beings by other living beings.

Producer

An organism in the trophic chain that is able to produce its own food on the basis of inorganic substances. Plants, on land, and algae, in water, are producer organisms and constitute the first level of trophic networks.

Savanna

A grassland in the tropical climate of the Southern Hemisphere. It is characterized by a scarcity of scattered trees, principally acacias and baobabs, and by a warm climate throughout the year, which alternates between a dry and a humid season.

Scientific Method

The process followed in scientific study to acquire verifiable knowledge. Although it may vary by discipline, it is based on some common principles: observation of the phenomena under study; formulation of a hypothesis; empirical verification through experimentation; analysis of the data obtained; and drawing some conclusions that can confirm or invalidate the hypothesis posed.

Semidesert

A more extensive and productive habitat than the desert and with more frequent precipitation (up to 16 inches [40 cm] a year), which allows a greater number of plants to grow. It may be hot year-round or else very cold in the winter.

Soil

The set of physical, chemical, and biological elements that make up the natural substrate in which life develops on the surface of the continents. It arises from the interaction between rocks and external agents.

Supralittoral

The marine littoral zone farthest from the tide's reach, which is never submerged under water.

Swamp

Area of stagnant water up to three feet (one meter) deep, which forms naturally as water accumulates in a depression in the ground. Swamps constitute habitats rich in plant life, and they produce a large amount of food for many animal species.

Symbiosis

A relationship of permanent association between two organisms of different species, which benefits at least one of them, with the other benefiting (mutualism), being harmed (parasitism), or being indifferent (commensalism).

Taiga

A coniferous forest in climates that are very cold and have strong winds; also called boreal forest. It is the most extensive expanse on the planet.

Territoriality

The tendency toward isolation of certain individuals imposing their domination over a territory.

Trophic Level

A species' position in the trophic, or food, chain, based upon the number of steps in which energy transfer has occurred. Producers make up the first level, followed by consumers and decomposers.

Tropical Forest

A forest found in warm and humid climates, near the Equator, characterized by a great variety of very tall trees, and a great variety of animal species.

Tundra

The region around the Arctic characterized by extreme cold, strong winds and the absence of trees. It has very poor soil, with a permanent layer of permafrost under the surface, and few plant species, such as grasses, mosses, lichens, and some shrubs.

Understory

The intermediate stratum of a forest, between the forest floor and the canopy, also called underbrush, which shelters shrubs, thickets, and climbing vines.

Index